These 3 Words

A 31-DAY DEVOTIONAL TO LIVE DEEPER IN THE WORDS OF JESUS

Aaron Hansel

Devotional Topics

Introduction

Words are powerful. Words have the power to build a person up or tear them down. Words have the power to excite or depress, create, or destroy. Words create values, define actions, and ultimately direct a person's life. Words have the ability to shape beliefs, provide hope and impart security. Yes, words have power.

When God created the heavens and the earth, He used words. Genesis Chapter 1 is dedicated to what God spoke into existence. Paul records in Colossians 1:16, *"For all things were created, in Heaven and on earth, visible and invisible, whether thrones or dominions or rulers or authorities—all things were created through Him and for Him."* His words spoke everything physical and spiritual into being. Think about the fact that "it was *through* Him and *for* Him that everything was created." This includes you, and this includes His words. Jesus' words have lost no power or authority today as they had when He spoke to creation.

The words of Jesus are a believer's source, direction, and wisdom needed to live life in accordance with God's will both *for us* and *in us*. If the words that hurt us the most are from the ones that are supposed to love us, envision the words spoken to you from the One who loves you the most – Jesus. The words of Jesus carry the authority to create new things, tear down the old, build up a person, supply the strength needed to live life, and provide a right worldview. The words of Jesus are powerful. The words of Jesus are purposeful. His words speak directly to us today.

His words are *authority*. Matthew 28:18, Jesus said, *"All authority is given unto Me in heaven and in earth."* All authority means that Jesus not only *has* but *is* all power. So, when Jesus speaks, He speaks supremely, with all authority because He is all authority and when Jesus speaks, incredible things happen.

His words *transform* lives. With a word, Jesus set the demoniac free (Matthew 8:28; Mark 5:1; Luke 8:26) and called Lazarus from the grave (John 11:11). His words transformed the lives of Nicodemus (John 3), the adulterous woman (John 8:2-11), and the Samaritan woman (John 4). The words of Jesus still transform people's lives today.

His words are *healing*. Whether it was with an individualized touch or commanding healing over a distance, when Jesus spoke the words of healing, it happened. In the case of the nobleman's son (John 4:46-54), and the healing of the centurion's servant (Matthew 8:5-13; Luke 7:1-10), Jesus healed by His words! From the people with leprosy that He healed (Matthew 8:1–4, Mark 1:40–45 and Luke 5:12–16) to the emotional distress of the Samaritan woman (John 4), it was the words of Jesus that brought healing, restoration, and transformation to their lives.

3 words. That is what this devotional is about. 3 words of Jesus to activate healing, transformation, greater intimacy and revelation of His love and Spirit. Each day of this devotional highlights 3 words of Jesus that will challenge greater growth and experience in our daily Christian life. The words of Jesus transformed my life many years ago, and my prayer is that His words will deeply transform your life and draw you into a deeper and closer relationship with Him.

Forward

"Words Matter". According to PsycheCentral; research has found that the choice of words can cause specific areas of the brain to activate, and can affect a person's subjective experience of pain. People use word associations to perceive neutral events as positive or negative. Words can hurt, but words can also heal. Our Lord Jesus Christ said in St John 6:63 "The words I speak to you, they are spirit and they are life". Meaning that the words that come from his lips are more than just typical words. They are "Spirit" – alluding to the incomparable effect of leading, and guiding our inner man that comes from his words. They are "Life" – alluding to the actual "Making Us Alive" or "Quickening" that comes from receiving his words in a spiritual manner. In other words, to take heed to the words that Jesus speaks offers spiritual guidance and leadership in this present life that will result in eternal life and peace with God.

The essence of this discourse of Our Lord is truly manifested and magnified in the powerful dynamics of this 31 day devotional that you are about to embark on *These 3 Words*. The author, Pastor Aaron Hansel has skillfully compiled a magnificent array of revelatory excellence in this compelling and relevant daily devotional that will enhance your biblical understanding, strengthen your appreciation for the word of scripture, and enlighten you in your personal daily application of the bible in real world situations. In fact, in reading *These 3 Words* on a daily basis I have found myself feeling challenged, and compelled to take inventory of my life holistically, and determining whether or not I am truly following the words of Our Lord wholeheartedly. This has led to a level of spiritual encouragement in my life that I have not experienced in my over 34 years of ministry.

I have worked with Pastor Hansel in ministry for nearly 20 years, and have found his commitment and dedication to the work of the Kingdom of God being infectious and encouraging. He is truly just one of those few Pastors that just always seems to have his priorities and hierarchy of needs in perfect congruence. God is always first; his family is a clear and resounding next, and then everything else in its place after.

This book; *These 3 Words*, are a microcosm of the life that he lives, and is quite in line with the ministry that Our Lord has placed within him. Pastor Hansel has a genuine concern for all mankind; however, he has a special burden for the less fortunate, underserved, less educated. The overtones of that specific burden is clear in the simplicity of the devotional. The power that is translated in only *Three Words* a day. Not complicated words, just extremely powerful words that literally anyone can understand

As I pondered *These 3 Words* for days on end, I informed Pastor Hansel that "with all due respect, it is absolutely impossible that you could have come up with the content for this treatise of your own thoughts and ideas. In other words; "flesh and blood could not have revealed this to you, but only our father who is in heaven."

These 3 Words is the most transformative and extraordinary daily devotional that I have encountered in over 34 years of ministry. Prepare your hearts, and minds to be stretched beyond the norm in order to receive revelation beyond the norm with just These 3 Words.

Dr. Michael H. Hatch
Balm of Gilead Global Ministries
Las Vegas, NV

Acknowledgements

"I believe that Aaron has truly captured the heart of Christ in this 31-day devotional, '*These 3 Words*.' I deeply appreciate the time taken by Pastor Aaron to remind us of the eternal words of our life changing King, Jesus Christ. These words are still able to enlighten and encourage those who desire to seek Christ with their whole heart. They will most certainly find him in '*These 3 Words*.'"

Pastor Deonita C. Atkinson
Kingdom Family International
Author of *Leadership of One*

"I absolutely love this devotional book. As we all know, a lot can happen in just 3 days, and Jesus consistently says powerful things in just 3 words. My friend, Aaron Hansel, draws out so much meaning and gives us all so much to contemplate and meditate on—in just 3 words!"

Pastor Randy Greer
Trinity Life Center, Las Vegas NV.

"*These 3 Words* is an incredible devotional that helps you see how the words of Jesus impacted humanity and still impact us today. Aaron analyzes how Jesus' words cause us to reflect on the deep meanings historically and personally through his insightful commentary."

Pastor Dean Sanner MFT
Discovery Church, North Las Vegas NV.

"*These 3 Words*", bring to light the simplicity and the depth of God's Word. Jesus often used few words to illustrate the treasures of the Word and challenge us to holy living. You will be blessed whether you're new to life in Jesus or you've been a follower for years. It's a great devo to share with a group!

Pastor Richard Box
Living Grace Foursquare Church, Las Vegas NV.

Dedication

This devotional is first and foremost dedicated to the glory of God. I sincerely pray that all who read and accept the challenges will have their faith in Christ realized into a greater and more personal reality.

This is also dedicated to my wife, Danita. I am so thankful for your continued love, support, and dedication. It is because of you that I am the man I am today. Thank you for marrying me!

I also dedicate this work to my two sons Isaac and Caleb. God incredibly blessed us to be your parents, and I hope that you will live every day of your life fully dedicated to Christ. There is no better journey in life than discovering the unlimited wonder of God.

How to best utilize this devotional

The purpose of this devotional is to encourage, deepen, and strengthen your faith in Christ.

- Commit a minimum of 5 minutes every day for 31 days to read a devotion.
- At the end of each devotion there is a *Consider* paragraph. This is for deeper personal reflection and life application.
- Following the *Consider* paragraph, there is a *Challenge* statement. The *Challenge* is designed for you to meditate on and live out the 3 words of Jesus for that day. For example: Day 22 is *"Feed my Sheep,"* there is a question asked in the *Challenge*; "Are you in a place where you are feeding God's sheep?" meaning are you discipling and helping others grow in their faith? This is a challenge to meditate on *These 3 Words* of Jesus and how you are living them out.
- Meditate and memorize the 3 words of Jesus for that day.
- This devotional is intended for personal devotions but can be used for small group study and for discipleship to further discuss and apply the truths presented each day.

DAY 1

"Come, follow me"

"Come, follow me," *Jesus said, "and I will send you out to fish for people."*

—Matthew 4:19

In Matthew 4 Jesus is walking by the sea of Galilee when he sees Peter and Andrew out fishing. Jesus extends 3 words; *"Come, follow me."* Those 3 words so powerfully impacted them that it caused such quick and decisive action that *"...they left their nets and followed him"* (v.20).

Soon the trio comes to James and John who were in their boat along with their father fixing their nets after a long day of fishing. Jesus called to them and *"...immediately they left the boat and their father and followed him"* (v.22). I am sure that in that moment, those fishermen had no idea how their lives were going to change, but their quick response demonstrates the power of Jesus's words as He won over their hearts.

At first, it may seem that Peter, Andrew, James, and John lost a lot in their decision to follow Jesus. The loss of their nets, their boats, and possible relationships meant the loss of business, income, family, and community status. Now Jesus' band of followers come to the tax collector Matthew where Jesus extends the same invitation.

"After this, Jesus went out and saw a tax collector by the name of Levi sitting at his tax booth. "Follow me," Jesus said to him, and Levi got up, left

everything and followed him" (Luke 5:27-28). Like the others Levi (Matthew) immediately left *everything* to follow Jesus. He gave up money, influence, power, and the position of a tax collector to follow Jesus. No questions, just commitment.

The thought of loss for some people today is a real hinderance to following Jesus. Loss of status, friendships, or "giving up the good life" has too much of a hold on the hearts of people to really understand that Jesus' command to *"Come, follow me"* is about *both* loss and gain. Paul says,

"You were taught, with regard to your former way of life, to put off your old self, which is being corrupted by its deceitful desires; to be made new in the attitude of your minds; and to put on the new self, created to be like God in true righteousness and holiness" (Ephesians 4:22-24). Paul is speaking of a break with the past, that life is dead along with all its deceitful desires and corruption. Jesus is the new life, not an addition to the old life.

Like the disciples, maybe you have "lost" things when you responded to those 3 words of Jesus, *"Come, follow me."* But think about what you have gained in Christ. Following Jesus means the "loss" of your old life, the sin, shame and guilt of past failures and mistakes.

These 3 words of Jesus, *"Come, follow me,"* is not a suggestive, occasional, or a casual command to hang out for a couple of hours once a week, but a call of commitment and a way of life that applies to every moment of every day.

These 3 words are the call every believer to experience the presence, knowledge, and will of God. How can a person know the will of God apart from the word of God? It is impossible. These 3 words, *"Come, follow me"* set a new course of life for these ordinary fishermen. Now, instead of fishing to make a living, they would soon *be fishing for people (v.19),* showing others that Jesus is the way to life.

These 3 words are the greatest personal invitation of God to all mankind! What a glorious invitation Jesus offers today! To lose the old destructive ways and patterns of life. To embrace a new life, completely free and forgiven of sin. A new life with a different direction and meaning.

Now that you have gained Christ, you have everything!

"Therefore, if anyone is in Christ, the new creation has come: The old has gone, the new is here!"

—*2 Corinthians 5:17*

⅄⅄⅄

Consider: Remember when you heard these 3 words of Jesus, *"Come, follow me."* How has your life changed since you responded to these 3 words? Consider what you have lost. Consider what you have gained in Christ. Do you know that there is no such thing as a "part time" follower of Jesus? Consider the fact that you have a personal relationship with God, a vibrant life of freedom and meaning as you embrace the call of God to follow Him. What is gained in Christ far outweighs what is lost in the world.

Challenge: Matthew does not record *why* they left everything to follow Jesus, but *how*. These future world changers immediately recognized and responded to the authority of Jesus' 3 words to *"Come, follow me."* Their hearts are so deeply impressed that they had to respond immediately.

When you are in your routines for the day, meditate on the 3 words; *"Come, follow me."* Think about the impact those words have had on your life and the lives of the disciples. Meditate on the scriptures that have helped shape your faith and grow in your love of God. Is there any area of your life that you need to follow Jesus more closely?

DAY 2

"I am willing"

> *"A man with leprosy came to him and begged him on his knees, 'If you are willing, you can make me clean.' Filled with compassion, Jesus reached out his hand and touched the man. "**I am willing**," he said. "Be clean!" Immediately the leprosy left him and he was cleansed."*
>
> *—Mark 1:40-42*

In Leviticus chapters 13-14, there are more than 100 verses dealing with a person who has leprosy. A person with leprosy would have an extremely difficult life. They would be exiled from the community, ostracized from society, and never be allowed to enter the Temple. A person with leprosy could never visit a home, never touch anyone, live in a quarantined area, and were forced to wear a face covering below the eyes. A person with leprosy would have no means to live, and would have to shout, "unclean, unclean!" when encountering another person on a road. People with leprosy endured terrible mental and physical anguish. In fact, William Barclay wrote, "It is a kind of terrible progressive death in which a man dies by inches" (1). E. W. G. Masterman writes: "No other disease reduces a human being for so many years to so hideous a wreck" (2).

It was against Jewish customs to greet a person with leprosy. A leper had to stay a minimum of 6 feet away from any other person, and 150 feet away if it was windy. Jewish historian Josephus said that lepers were treated "as if they were, in effect, dead men" (3). Leprous people were considered judged by God because of their sin. The life of a leper meant being untouched, unloved, undesirable, and unsavable. There were no illusions of a leper's life, there is no hiding the condition or concealing their fate. Life was very difficult.

That all changes with 3 words of Jesus. These 3 words, *"I am willing"* so powerfully demonstrate the love, compassion, and desire of God for people, no matter what the situation. Despite this man's condition and experiences, he came to Jesus in faith, reverence, and humility. *"If you are willing..."* may seem like words of uncertainty, or insecurity, but the point is that this man came to Jesus! It is truly a humble, contrite heart that is hopeful in faith that finds the touch of God.

Faith does not deny reality. Faith is the choice to press into God, to keep pursuing His presence, to keep rehearsing His promises, to keep on asking, seeking, and knocking despite the realities faced each day. Faith is trusting in God that He has the best plan even when we do not see or understand the situations we face. Faith is confidence and resting in the peace of His promises and holding the right perspectives as we navigate life's twists and turns. Timothy Keller is quoted as saying, "If you say: I believed in God, I trusted God and He didn't come through – You only trusted God to meet your agenda" (4). Faith is the assurance that God will act on His Word, fulfilling His work in your life.

Think about the weight of these 3 words, *"I am willing."* No matter what sin, sickness, or area of life you need Jesus to reach out and touch, He is willing. Breaking away from social norms, ridicule and rejection, the leper came to Jesus in faith, reverence, and humility – that took some faith!

This man's defining moment in life was not in the sickness, or in the sin others labeled him with, it was in the power of Jesus' healing touch. Imagine the gasp of the onlookers as Jesus touched him. Not only was Jesus touching someone who was deemed untouchable and loving someone unlovable, Jesus should have contracted that man's disease as soon as He touched him. He did not. As Matthew 8:17 points out, "This was to fulfill what was spoken through the prophet Isaiah: "He took up our infirmities and bore our diseases." Now this man is restored to his family and welcomed back to the community.

These 3 words of Jesus capture the heart and desire of God to touch lives today. The issue is not with Jesus. The issue is about our faith, reverence, and humility in approaching with our needs. Jesus turns no one away! He is willing!

> *"Great crowds came to him, bringing the lame, the blind, the crippled, the mute and many others, and laid them at his feet; and he healed them."*
>
> *—Matthew 15:30*

⅄ ⅄ ⅄

Consider: What a powerful illustration of our Lord's power in Mark chapter 1. The accounts are also in Matthew chapter 8, and Luke 5. Consider the fact that Jesus could have spoken to the disease and the man would have been healed, but *Jesus touched him*. When Jesus touches a person's life, that life will change. Whatever the need may be, whether it's physical, emotional, or extenuating circumstances, *Jesus is willing*. No one is so "unclean" that they are beyond the touch of Jesus. Nothing can separate us from the love of God. Consider the approach of the leper's faith, reverence, and humility when he approached Jesus; consider Jesus and His loving response. Lives change at the touch of God.

Challenge: It was probably many years since this man has been touched, or able to hold his wife or children, or to joke around with friends or go to the temple to worship. He was isolated and alone, and now he is healed and restored. Meditate on these words of Jesus: *"I am willing."* What areas of your life, family, or circumstances do you need the touch of God in? How is your faith challenged by this man's faith?

1. Barclay, William. The Daily Study Bible: Matthew Vol.1. Westminster Press. Philadelphia PA. 1975 p.295.
2. Ibid. p.295.
3. Ibid. p.295.
4. Keller, Timothy. 2014. @timkellernyc: Twitter. https://mobile.twitter.com/timkellernyc/status/541331745313148928?lang=id.

DAY 3

"It is written"

> *"**It is written**: 'Man shall not live on bread alone, but on every word that comes from the mouth of God.'"*
>
> *—Matthew 4:4*

We all will face battles in life. This is a part of the Christian faith. In fact, faith will not be strengthened, deepened, or proven for us until it is tested in battle. If you are breathing, you are battling. For some people, life is a daily battle of physical challenges, emotional tensions, relational issues, and let's not forget the thought life. Oh, the wars that rage in the mind! Rarely do the battles we face come from one direction. They surge at our weakest moments, and like waves pounding the shore, they are constant and unrelenting.

After 40 days of fasting, Jesus was physically weak and hungry. The devil does not approach Jesus when He is feeling good and strong, he comes at a time of weakness and hunger. The devil does not temp for the sake of tempting. The devil comes with *intent* in the temptations. The *intent* of the devil is to cause doubt leading to denial with the main goal of derailing faith in God. If Satan tried this with Jesus, be sure that he will try it with you. Three ways the devil tempted Jesus to doubt and deny God with intent to derail Him as recorded in Matthew are:

1. *Turn stones into bread* – Doubt and deny God's ability to provide. (Matthew 4:3)
2. *Jump from the pinnacle of the temple so the angels could save Him* – Doubt and deny God's ability to protect. (Matthew 4:5-6)
3. *Bow down and worship the devil in exchange for power* – Doubt and deny God's supreme authority and glory. (Matthew 4:8-9)

The devil came at Jesus with precision. He wanted Jesus to doubt and deny God's power, to worship creation rather than the Creator and to shift His desires from pleasing God by appealing to His human nature to please self. This is a working game plan the devil has used for centuries. Preoccupation with self, self-pleasure and self-reliance will invalidate the grace and mercy God extends to His people, simply because life and devotion becomes about the worship of self and not God.

Jesus defeated each temptation with 3 powerful words; *"It is written."* These three words are the sword of the Spirit! *"It is written,"* needs to be in the heart, on the mind, and in the mouth of every believer, every time temptation tries to redirect faith from pleasing God to focus on self. The Word of God was Jesus' source of victory and His source of strength for defeating the illicit temptations that He faced. God's Word is still an undeniable force relevant to every need we have, every battle we face, and can win the unrelenting war raging in our minds.

Colossians 3:16 states, "Let the message about Christ, in all its richness, fill your lives" (NLT). In a sermon preached by Charles Spurgeon he spoke, "Do try, dear friends, to get so full of 'the word of Christ' in all forms of it, that you may run over with it. You know, it cannot come out of you if it is not first in you" (1). Change on the outside first begins on the inside. The Word of God is where Jesus found victory and it is where we will find victory as well. Jesus found victory in seeking the Father, selflessly giving to others, and living out God's Word, not to Himself, but to God first.

> *"I have told you these things, so that in me you may have peace. In this world you will have trouble. But take heart! I have overcome the world."*
>
> —*John 16:33*

⅄⅄⅄

Consider: No one is exempt from temptations in life. However, these 3 words of Jesus, *"it is written..."* show the way to victory in the temptations we face. Consider your life and the temptations you face. Jesus' victory over temptation was drawing from the Word of God. Consider the Scriptures that can provide you with the strength, wisdom, and power to defeat the devil when he tries to sow doubt, denial or outright derail your faith.

Challenge: Outside of God, you know yourself better than anyone else. You know your weaknesses and temptations. Meditate on these 3 words of Jesus, *"it is written..."* throughout your day today. What are the specific scriptures in your arsenal where you have found your strength, wisdom, or guidance? What Scriptures are your sword when temptation comes, or help mold your thoughts and bring you peace in battle? Are these scriptures memorized? This is an encouragement so when that foe of temptation rises and tears away at your thought life and seeks to redirect the course of your attitudes and actions, you can simply respond like Jesus by saying, *"It is written..."*

1. Intended for reading on the Lord's Day, June 17th, 1900. Delivered by C.H. Spurgeon at the Metropolitan Tabernacle, Newington, April 10th 1881. https://www.preceptaustin.org/spurgeon_on_colossians_2#ciw

DAY 4

"Repent and believe"

> *"The time has come," he said. "The kingdom of God has come near.* ***Repent and believe*** *the good news!"*
>
> —*Mark 1:15*

This verse opens with Jesus saying, *"The time has come,"* indicating that God's appointed Messiah has arrived, and God's redemptive promises are in effect. This was the hour; this was the time for the realization that the long-awaited Messiah was in their midst and the Kingdom of heaven was near. It was time for the revelation and message of Jesus to the world. John's message of repentance pointed to Christ and prepared the way for Jesus. His message is that salvation is now here, and He is that message.

Our hour of realization is now. These 3 words of Jesus, *"repent and believe,"* afford for us an opportunity to realize and receive grace, mercy, and the love of God at deeper and more personal levels. Repentance often carries a negative connotation to it, conjuring up images of a disheveled man standing on a streetcorner, or a craggy old preacher demanding penance and making amends for sins. In reality, repentance is a gift of God that allows us to realize and change areas in our life and draw closer to God.

Repentance comes from the Greek word *metanoia.* At its root, repentance is about change. A change of mind to realign our heart, desires, thoughts, values, actions, and attitudes with God's. Repentance is God's work of grace to bring freedom from guilt, shame, and regret and to set a new course for life without the sin that easily entangles. In military terms, *metanoia* could be used to mean an "about-face." Soldiers marching in one direction swiftly turn and march in the other direction. This is what we do; instead of marching toward destruction and our own sinful desires, we about-face and march toward God and pursue His desires. The only way to turn from sin is to turn toward Christ.

The first step in becoming a Christian involves *metanoia* and without it, you will not know Christ the way you are called to know Him. Repentance and belief initiate salvation. They bring the change that we need and God desires. This work of the Holy Spirit brings change in our mind about who Christ is *to* us, His work *in* us, and our life *for* Him. When true repentance is practiced, the grace of God is more realized, and change is effective.

The word for believe comes from the Greek word *pisteuo*. It means to accept as genuine and real and being worthy of complete trust. It is about receiving the truth of who Jesus is and the activity of the Holy Spirit working in our lives bringing the truth of the gospel into hearts. Belief will be evidenced by obedience and by the good fruit produced in accordance with the gospel.

The truth of the gospel demands a response from the believer. Jesus' 3 words, *"repent and believe"* is the response demanded. Breaking off past agreements with sin and making the choice to turn to Christ brings freedom and ushers in the new life. A change of life brings new levels of belief. Remember the freedom and joy when you first received Christ as Lord and Savior? How have you seen your life change as you repented and received the grace of God for the things that once held you captive? This change brought faith and greater belief in the realization of Jesus. Do you remember the joy of knowing your sins were forgiven and the passion you had to know Jesus and read the Word? Remember the realization of God's grace and love you felt? That is the effect of *metanoia* and the work of *pisteuo*.

> *"Jesus answered, "I am the way and the truth and the life. No one comes to the Father except through me."*
>
> *—John 14:6*

⅄ ⅄ ⅄

Consider: The truth of the Gospel demands a response. The hour of realization is today, do not let this pass you by. Is there any area of your life where you need to follow the words of Jesus and *"repent and believe?"* Repentance is about receiving mercy, grace, and love. Repentance is about experiencing a new life filled with purpose. Belief is about the realization and trustworthiness of Christ and producing good fruit.

Challenge: Repentance and belief are about recognition and growth. Meditate on these 3 words of Jesus. Look back on your salvation experience and times of joy in Christ. Remember the passion and the desires you had for worship, prayer, and service? Remember the areas of life that God has brought about change? What a difference *metanoia* makes as you continue this process. If we fail to depend on the Spirit's enabling power and strength to turn from sin and believe the promises of God to destroy the deceitfulness of the devil, then we sin and will not achieve God's desires for us. What areas of your life require repentance and belief?

DAY 5

"I tell you"

> *"Which is easier: to say to this paralyzed man, 'Your sins are forgiven,' or to say, 'Get up, take your mat and walk'? But I want you to know that the Son of Man has authority on earth to forgive sins." So he said to the man,* ***"I tell you,*** *get up, take your mat and go home." He got up, took his mat and walked out in full view of them all. This amazed everyone and they praised God, saying, "We have never seen anything like this!"*
>
> *—Mark 2:9-12*

If you see the slogan "Just do it," what do you think of? Nike shoes and apparel, right? If you hear the phrase "I'm lovin' it" what does your mind think of? McDonalds, right? The three words in these and other slogans are so ingrained into our society that once we see or hear them our minds automatically associate the phrase with the product. Hearing the same thing over and over helps you remember and build association with a person, product, or idea.

In Matthew's account of the Sermon on the Mount, Jesus speaks the words *"I tell you"* at least 13 times. Why? Jesus wants us to know truth and the standard of truth. When Jesus speaks these 3 words *"I tell you,"* He speaks as the authority of God and the authority of Scripture. His words emphasize His deity and seek to align people to His will. Believers may live *in* the world, but are not called to be *of* the world, or to live according to the standards and expectations of secular society. Believers are different, called to a higher standard of conduct and character.

For example, Matthew 5:44 *"But **I tell you**, love your enemies and pray for those who persecute you."* Jesus wants us to love and pray for those that persecute and hate believers. This is a higher call of Jesus we are to function in. Loving those that do not love you reflects the character of God.

How about Matthew 6:25, *"Therefore **I tell you**, do not worry about your life, what you will eat or drink; or about your body, what you will wear. Is not life more than food, and the body more than clothes?"* Believers are not called to worry, fret or fear. Of course, this does not negate the responsibilities of believers but calls the believer to a higher level of trust and faith in God. Worrying about life seeks to replace the trust we place in the One who directs life.

One more, Matthew 5:28 *"But **I tell you** that anyone who looks at a woman lustfully has already committed adultery with her in his heart."* The condition of the heart is a consistent target of Jesus' teaching. The meditation of the heart and mind can harbor sin just as much as conduct and words. These 3 words of Jesus call believers to a higher standard of integrity and conduct than the world.

Throughout the entire gospel, Jesus continually uses the phrase *"I tell you,"* as a way of inspiring His readers to live at a level greater than the world standards; not only in their outward actions but their inward attitudes and motivations of heart. No wonder the realization of Jesus' words to the people were, *"When Jesus had finished saying these things, the crowds were amazed at his teaching, because he taught as one who had authority, and not as their teachers of the law" (Mark 1:22).*

In Mark 2, Jesus tells the paralytic *to get up, take your mat and go home,* and he did it. When you read the 3 words of Jesus, *"I tell you"* – Just do it! Believers are incompatible with worldly means and values. Jesus is calling you to a higher standard of living, life, and love.

"Sanctify them by the truth; your word is truth."

—John 17:17

Consider: The 3 words of Jesus *"I tell you"* are powerfully authoritative and necessary for believers to pay attention to. Followers of Christ are called to live at a different standard than the world with different beliefs, and values. Jesus' 3 words *"I tell you"* are key to living out successful obedience to Christ.

Challenge: Think about all the Scriptures above and other Scriptures where Jesus says, *"I tell you."* Meditate on each Scripture and think about the authority of Christ, the power demonstrated, and the direction given in His 3 words *"I tell you."* The man in Mark 2:9-12 obeyed Christ and was healed. Remember that Jesus lifts people, sin lowers people, so raise your standards of life, do not lower them to the world.

DAY 6

"I ask you"

> *"But Jesus knew what they were thinking and said to the man with the shriveled hand, "Get up and stand in front of everyone." So he got up and stood there. Then Jesus said to them, "**I ask you**, which is lawful on the Sabbath: to do good or to do evil, to save life or to destroy it?" He looked around at them all, and then said to the man, "Stretch out your hand." He did so, and his hand was completely restored."*
>
> —*Luke 6:8-10*

These 3 words of Jesus are part of yet seemingly another confrontation with the religious leaders. In this passage of Scripture, the Pharisees did not come to church to draw close to God or worship Him. They came to church that day with an intent to "trap" and accuse Jesus. However, Jesus knows the desire and intention of every heart, in fact, the word for *thinking* (v.8) is more literally *reasonings* which implies that Jesus already knew their schemes and plans to trap Him.

Possibly, this paralyzed man was a "plant" by the Pharisees knowing that Jesus would likely heal the man, thus giving the Pharisees an opportunity to bring accusations against Jesus for breaking their religious laws. It is sad to think that the Pharisees would use such a man, who is in obvious need, for their own deviant schemes. This shows one of many reasons why Jesus continually confronts them. They look upon and treated this man as well as others with disdain and disrespect, totally disregarding that this man needed ministry.

Jesus calls the man front and center of everyone and confronts the religious leaders with 3 powerful words, *"I ask you."* These 3 words of Jesus *point back to Himself* as having greater authority than the Pharisee's laws and traditions. He is asking them if it is right and good to heal on the Sabbath. It is always good to do good, so Jesus completely heals the man.

"I ask you" are 3 words that Jesus uses to confront us today. When we become believers, Jesus begins to work in us, to root out the worldly thoughts, desires and actions that are contrary to His Word. One of God's ultimate goals is to transform and conform us into the image of Christ, to be renewed in spirit and thought all for His glory. Jesus' 3 words *"I ask you"* summons each person to a greater reality of His authority in our life today. Think about how Jesus confronts us:

Jesus confronts our religion by asking us to be in a relationship with Him. Jesus confronts our selfishness by asking us to be selfless. Jesus confronts our inabilities by asking us to trust in His ability. Jesus confronts our pride by asking us to be humble. Jesus confronts our hurts by asking us to forgive and not to take revenge. Jesus confronts our doubts and asks us to believe in faith. Jesus confronts our weakness by asking us to find strength in Him. Jesus confronts our heart and desires by asking us to love Him first and He will meet our needs. Yes, Jesus is confronting every believer today with 3 powerful words, *"I ask you"* and our response will determine the depth of our relationship and the reality of our faith and trust in Him.

What is Jesus asking of you today? It is comforting to know that when Jesus confronts us, it is in love and with a purpose to draw us closer to Him, to reveal His greater plan and purpose for our life. It is good when Jesus confronts us.

"Everything is possible for one who believes."

—*Mark* 9:23

⅄⅄⅄

Consider: Jesus confronts us with 3 words. *"I tell you."* What do these 3 words mean to you? What is Jesus confronting in your life? How will you choose to respond? Consider the words of Martin Luther *"Faith is a living and unshakable confidence, a belief in the grace of God so assured that a man would die a thousand deaths for its sake."* The Pharisees were so caught up in their religion and self-righteousness that they missed the opportunity to minister to this man who was in obvious need.

Challenge: In prayer today, meditate on these 3 words of Jesus and allow His loving presence to bring healing or freedom to the areas of your life He is *"telling you"* about. There is great love when Jesus confronts us, He loves you and desires to demonstrate that love both to you and in you. It is because Jesus loves us so intensely that He confronts us with such powerful words as *"I tell you."*

DAY 7

"Do you believe"

> *"As Jesus went on from there, two blind men followed him, calling out, "Have mercy on us, Son of David!" When he had gone indoors, the blind men came to him, and he asked them, "**Do you believe** that I am able to do this?" "Yes, Lord," they replied. Then he touched their eyes and said, "According to your faith let it be done to you."*
>
> —*(Matthew 9:27-29)*

Do you believe? These 3 words of Jesus drive to the very core of a person's faith and belief. This is quite possibly the most important question that is asked of every person, but so much more important is the response to these 3 words. Jesus asked His disciples the same core question in Matthew 16:13-16:

> *"When Jesus came to the region of Caesarea Philippi, he asked his disciples, "Who do people say the Son of Man is?" They replied, "Some say John the Baptist; others say Elijah; and still others, Jeremiah or one of the prophets." "But what about you?" he asked. "Who do you say I am?" Simon Peter answered, "You are the Messiah, the Son of the living God."*

What about you, who do you say Jesus is? The response to that question lies in faith.

The Scripture records that there were two blind men, maybe they were father and son, brothers or two friends bonded by their blindness and partnered together to survive the difficulties a life of begging required. These two blind men *followed* Jesus. Perhaps someone was leading them, or they were following the noise of the crowd and the clamoring of others for His attention, yet they followed Jesus. It is amazing that two physically blind men had clear vision as to who Jesus is. They could not see, but they had faith, and it was their faith to which Jesus responded.

The religious leaders could not see what these two blind men saw, in fact, "the people of Galilee are depicted *as blind*, aimless, and distressed. They are *blind to who Jesus is*. They are *blind* to His kingdom. They are *blind* to their own sin. They are *blind* to what *Jesus* offers them. They are *blind* to how they should live. And they are *blind* to what distresses them. The people, like these *two blind* beggars, are in desperate need *of mercy from the Son of David to open their eyes* to the reality of the gospel" (1). We all need our eyes open to the greater reality and power of the gospel!

When Jesus brings the two men indoors, possibly to quiet down the attention being drawn to Him by their constant calling out, Jesus does not ask about their blindness. He does not ask about how they became this way or the people responsible. He asks about their faith. *"Do you believe that I am able to do this?"* It is not their condition that Jesus addresses, but their faith in Him. He showed the two men mercy and rewarded them with their sight according to their faith (v.29). It is about faith in Him – not knowledge about Him.

Jesus does work in our daily lives and knows our deepest needs. Jesus structured this demonstration of His healing power as validation that it is faith in Him that is paramount. As Oswald Chambers said, "Faith never knows where it is being led, but it loves and knows the One Who is leading" (2). The two men responded to the question of Jesus with a simple, "Yes Lord." How simple a response that warranted a mighty miracle.

These 3 words of Jesus, *"Do you believe..."* challenges a response. Sometimes it is pain, sickness, fear or frustration that drives us to Jesus and this is ok, but it is not the conditions or circumstances that He will address, it will be faith. "Do you believe that I am able to do this" is an invitation to strengthen our faith and deepen our trust in Him. All we need to do is respond with a "Yes Lord!"

> *"And without faith it is impossible to please Him, for he who comes to God must believe that He is and that He is a rewarder of those who seek Him."*
>
> —*Hebrews 11:6*

⅄⅄⅄

Consider: John 20:31 reminds us, *"But these are written that you may believe that Jesus is the Messiah, the Son of God, and that by believing you may have life in his name."* This reminds us that the gospel is about faith in Jesus and He is the message of hope, healing, and salvation that the world desperately needs to hear. Consider the 3 words of Jesus... *Do you believe,* and how those words have challenged and deepened your faith and relationship with Him.

Challenge: Meditate on these 3 words of Jesus today. How does the account of the two blind men challenge your faith? These men followed Jesus despite having no sight. The religious leaders were blind to the message, yet they could see perfectly. One of the greatest hindrances of people coming to faith in Christ is religion and sometimes their own circumstances. How are you responding to the circumstances in your life that are challenging to your faith?

1. Quote retrieved from: https://thebiblesays.com/commentary/matt/matt-9/matthew-927-31/
2. Chambers, Oswald. *My Utmost for His Highest.* Retrieved from: https://utmost.org/quotes/2315/.

DAY 8

"Love the Lord"

> *"**Love the Lord** your God with all your heart and with all your soul and with all your mind and with all your strength."*
>
> —*Mark* 12:30

These 3 words of Jesus, to *"love the Lord"* is the greatest command given to His followers. Our greatest call is to *love God first presently and actively* and above all because God can be compared to no one or nothing. He is to be loved above all other loves, all other desires, and all other "things" the world may offer. God desires that we love Him with the very core of our being, with our deepest affections, intellect, and understanding. Spiritual maturity is not just in acquiring Biblical knowledge, but it is a present tense reality discovered in these 3 words of Jesus.

To *"love the Lord"* sets all other loves in order. It is good to love and be passionate about recreation, family, sports, and other things, but as great as these things are, they are not to possess the primary position or hold top priority in our heart. That place is solely reserved for God.

1 John 4:16, *"And so we know and rely on the love God has for us. God is love. Whoever lives in love lives in God, and God in him."*

We love God by abiding in Him. John rightly says that, *"Whoever lives in love, lives in God."* This is not about acquiring facts about God; this is the place to live. A life of love must have a source from which that love flows. God is love; He is to be our Source to live out a life of love – not what the world calls "love," but God's love.

We are the testimony of God's love to this broken and dark world. The way we abide in Christ has a direct correlation to the way we love others and ourselves. The first commandment Jesus gives to "love God" *guarantees* the second command to *"love others."* How are we going to love others and lead others to Christ if we first do not seize and live out the love He gives? Love is realized by the intimate call of unity with Christ. His love seeks to deeply encounter every aspect of our mind, will, and emotions. His love is the standard for life. This is the display the world needs; the love of God in you. People will know the love of God by how you love them and by how He loves you.

These 3 words of Jesus are tremendously powerful. Do you know that God desires you more than you desire Him? Jesus said that we are to love the Lord *your* God. The word *"your"* is about possession. He possesses us because of His amazing grace. We possess Him as our ultimate source of good, hope, and strength. What God really wants from us is to love Him. We can obey God without loving Him, but if we love Him, obedience is a delight. Loving God will arm us against all the other things in life that will compete and rival for the top spot in our heart.

God has amazing dreams for you and your life. God desires that His love deeply encounter every area of your life. His love is the anchor of the soul, so when fears, insecurities, and doubt come, and they will, we abide in Him with an undivided mind and secure emotions. The more you taste His love, the more you desire His love.

> *"Taste and see that the LORD is good; blessed is the one who takes refuge in him."*
>
> —*Psalm 34:8*

Consider: God's love towards us is perfect and His fullest expression of love is in Jesus. Consider the cross of Christ. It was because God loves us so deeply that He was willing to allow Jesus to be crucified. Consider 1 John 4:9, "God showed how much he loved us by sending his one and only Son into the world so that we might have eternal life through him" (NLT).

As you draw closer to Jesus you draw closer to the love of God. It has been said that "you are the only Bible unbelievers will read." How do people read your life and love for God? How is God's love realized in your life?

Challenge: Meditate on these 3 words of Jesus today. This call of Jesus is for an unhindered commitment to God with a dedicated heart. In reality there is no way you can love God by your own efforts. This call of love is found by surrendering, submitting, and depending on the Holy Spirit to invigorate this love. How powerful is the love of God in you? Is it a reality of unhindered commitment and an experience of security and realized desire?

DAY 9

"Hunger and thirst"

> *"Blessed are those who* ***hunger and thirst*** *for righteousness, for they will be filled."*
>
> *—Matthew 5:6*

When you read the Sermon on the Mount (Matthew 5-7), you have a description of what every Christian is meant to be. The teachings of Jesus in the Sermon on the Mount are complete. They are not separated or divided but are the standard every believer is called to. One person cannot be a "peacemaker" and not be "meek," or one cannot be "poor in spirit" and not be "pure in heart." These principles may manifest themselves differently or certain ones may be stronger than others in a person's life, but they are all there and they are unified not divided. The great news is that each operation of Jesus' teaching is produced by the grace of God and is a work of the Holy Spirit in our life.

These 3 words of Jesus *"hunger and thirst"* are the catalyst for the fulfillment of the other *"blessed are those"* statements of Jesus in the beatitudes. His 3 words *"hunger and thirst"* are not meant as a "take it or leave it" attitude, but rather a daily "must have" like food and water. What draws your spiritual attention forms your spiritual appetites. If there is to be any starting point to fulfill the teachings of Jesus given in the Sermon on the Mount, it must be what we *"hunger and thirst"* for.

In Biblical times, food and water were not as plentiful as it is today, people were often hungry and thirsty. Hunger is a powerful force, in fact a recent *Forbes* article stated that *"Hunger Beats Fear as Natures Strongest Motivator"* (1).

Massive crowds followed Jesus to get a meal to meet their need. Their physical hunger and physical needs drove them to move wherever Jesus was going. Jesus then teaches that people are to hunger and thirst for righteousness, re-directing their desire for temporal food by prioritizing the need for spiritual righteousness.

A follower of Jesus is to be motivated and hungry for righteousness. Yes, the desires of the world are strong, but the deeper hunger of the soul where life's destiny is determined and God's work is manifested, is only satisfied by God's righteousness. We are created to *hunger and thirst.* God does not ask us to deny these desires for good things, however, true satisfaction is in intimate communion with Jesus himself, and there He will satisfy the deepest longings of our souls.

Multitudes flock to churches each week wearing "Christian masks" that hide the reality of their appetites and true intentions. For some, church is not for Jesus but for show, status, or some sort of social position. For others, church is a place of community, growth, and love where they gather with friends to worship the Lord. What would the church be like if believers came to service hungry for God's presence, hungry for an encounter with the Holy Spirit, not worrying about what Jesus can do for them but to simply be with Him? In *Diamonds in the Dust*, Joni Eareckson Tada insightfully writes, *"To hunger is to be human, but to hunger for God is to feed on Him. Hunger and thirst after His righteousness and feed on Him in your heart. Taste and see that the Lord is good; it is He who will fill you to satisfaction"* (2).

Jesus' 3 words *"hunger and thirst"* for righteousness describes a desperation in one's heart and soul that will not be satisfied with a trifling knowledge of God or a minimal improvement in moral conduct. It is unrelenting passion for the presence of God and will not look to be satisfied with an hour on Sunday. The hungry heart is a place Jesus longs to fill.

"Let us hold unswervingly to the hope we profess, for he who promised is faithful."

—Hebrews 10:23

⅄⅄⅄

Consider: Hunger is a powerful motivator. What you hunger and thirst for reveals the character and intent of your heart. Only you and God know what you are truly hungry for. Do you wear a "Christian mask" or know all the right "Christian words" to say on Sunday morning but really want to be somewhere else?

Challenge: Meditate on these 3 words of Jesus. Pray and examine the hunger and desires of your heart. Is Church a duty or a delight? Is being with Christ a passionate desire or a passive aversion? Think about the righteousness that God is calling you to and desires for you – are you hungry for that? Are you at a place in life that your hunger and thirst for the daily presence of God is as important as your daily need for food and water?

1. https://www.forbes.com/sites/jvchamary/2016/09/30/hungry-motivation/?sh=1f26fb8b5839
2. Tada, Joni Eareckson. *Diamonds in the Dust: 366 Sparkling Devotions.* Grand Rapids Michigan. Zondervan. 1993. Np.

DAY 10

"Who touched me?"

When she heard about Jesus, she came up behind him in the crowd and touched his cloak, [28] *because she thought, "If I just touch his clothes, I will be healed." Immediately her bleeding stopped and she felt in her body that she was freed from her suffering. At once Jesus realized that power had gone out from him. He turned around in the crowd and asked, "Who touched my clothes?" "You see the people crowding against you," his disciples answered, "and yet you can ask,* ***'Who touched me?'"***

—Mark 5:27-31

Hope is powerful. Hope offers the possibility of a better future. Hope supplies courage to face difficult situations. Hope infuses a person with expectation, raises longing in the heart, and anticipates freedom when circumstances seem dim, discouraging or disheartening. In fact, research says that hope can help us manage stress, anxiety, and even help cope with adversity. Research also indicates that hope contributes to our well-being, happiness, and motivates people to positive action. Yes, hope is powerful.

This woman in Mark 5 is a hero of hope. She is a woman with a medical issue that is seemingly incurable. G. Campbell Morgan says, "By the very law of her people, she was divorced from her husband and could not live in her home; she was ostracized from all society and must not come into contact with her old friends; she was excommunicated from the services of the synagogue, and thus shut out from the women's courts in the temple" (1). Much like the leper, she would have lived as an outcast, rejected, and shunned by society. Morgan continues, "Twelve years of agony, physical, mental, spiritual, in which she had poured out her wealth in the attempt to regain her health, with no success," (2) that is, until Jesus walks by.

Imagine how her hope soared when she heard Jesus was in town. For 12 years this woman possessed a hope that one day she would be healed. Now that hope is realized. Mark 5:24 says *"... a large crowd followed and pressed around him (Jesus)."* This crowd was so large that they were packed in the street, pressing around Jesus. It would have been very difficult for this woman to walk forward let alone to navigate through the crowd to touch Jesus. She could not just say, "Excuse me, I am unclean, I would like to touch Jesus' cloak," or, "Can I just get through to just touch His tassel, thank you."

What we need to catch is this. Many people were on the street "bumping" into Jesus that day, but this woman touched God. Maybe it was fear, shame or insecurity that kept her from facing Jesus, but it was her faith that touched Him. Like all of us, this woman's faith was imperfect, but the object of her faith was perfect. Jesus, as the object of our faith, is much more important than the quality of our faith. Not everyone has the same level of faith, but it is faith, no matter what degree, that Jesus responds to. That's when powerful things can happen in our lives. It's not the quantity of faith we profess, but the quality of faith in whom we possess that makes all the difference.

People by the thousands come to church each week and "bump" into Jesus, but there are few who touch God. 2 Corinthians 6:17 says, *"come out and be separate from them..."* You are not to be part of the crowd; you are to reach out and touch God. This woman's hope was realized in faith when she, despite her circumstances, reached out and touched Jesus. When Jesus said these 3 words, *"Who touched me?"* this woman, this completely rejected woman, was now the center of attention of possibly thousands of people.

Jesus was not mad at her or upset that she touched Him. He stopped the whole procession to address this woman's hope and faith!

> *"Now faith is confidence in what we hope for and assurance about what we do not see."*
>
> —*Hebrews 11:1*

⅄⅄⅄

Consider: "Bumping" into Jesus each week is not the same as touching God. Hope is not an "I wish for something to happen." Hope is an anchor for life that solidifies faith in the things to come. Hebrews 6:19a says, *"We have this hope as an anchor for the soul, firm and secure."* The promises of God, the faithfulness of God, the love and personal relationship possessed with God serve as an anchor of the soul for the storms we all will face in life.

Challenge: Meditate on these 3 words of Jesus and the faith of this woman. How does her faith challenge yours? Her faith was imperfect, like all of ours, but having Christ as the object of her faith secured her healing. In your situations in life remember; it is not about the quantity of faith we profess to have but the quality of our faith in Christ that makes all the difference.

1. Quoted from; https://www.swartzentrover.com/cotor/EBooks/holiness/Morgan/Mark/GAM_11.htm
2. Ibid.

DAY 11

"Come with Me"

*"Then, because so many people were coming and going that they did not even have a chance to eat, he said to them, "**Come with me** by yourselves to a quiet place and get some rest."*

—Mark 6:31

Life is busy. Life is demanding. For many people even when there is an opportunity to disconnect from the pressures of life, the mind wanders back to the "to do" list that demands our attention. Our finding *real* rest for some seems to be an impossible task but can be found in these 3 words of Jesus, *"Come with Me."* What a great invitation He offers to us. This is an invitation to get away *with* Him, not *from* Him, and enter a rest that is truly physically and spiritually rejuvenating and recuperating.

Jesus tells us to come to Him. Not to a church, doctrine, or denomination but *to Him personally*. Jesus is the source of peace and rest we long for. One moment with Jesus is worth more than a lifetime of effort. Oswald Chambers said that "Personal contact with Jesus alters everything" (1). True. Chambers also noted that, "The attitude of coming is that the will resolutely lets go of everything and deliberately commits all to Him" (2). What a powerful thought that one can let go of everything and get away with Jesus.

The greater the demands are on your life, the greater these words *"come with Me"* need to be activated and practiced. Learning to let go and commit all to Him may be easier said than done, however, when initiated, the burdens of life get lighter not heavier. Being committed and busy is not a bad thing, as long as our busyness does not realign the first and greatest call on our lives; intimacy with Christ. No amount of work will fulfill what intimacy in Christ offers.

These 3 words *"come with Me"* is an invitation for us to a place of trust, knowing that the work that needs to be done will get accomplished. Just 3 small but powerful words, *"come to Me"* is an invitation to a place where the Word of God will guide, inspire, and give insight into the life we live. Every Christian needs to accept this invitation. It is important that we get alone from time to time to hear God's voice and refresh ourselves physically and mentally.

Matthew 11:28-30 says, *"Come to me, all you who are weary and burdened, and I will give you rest. Take my yoke upon you and learn from me, for I am gentle and humble in heart, and you will find rest for your souls. For my yoke is easy and my burden is light."*

The more we "come away with" Christ, the more we realize how much we need Him. The more we need Him the more we desire Him. The more we desire Him the more we realize that everything is in Christ and He will take care of everything in our lives.

These 3 words of Jesus are a continual request to bring every trial, every trouble, and every conflict to Him. This will unburden our minds, and we will find rest for our souls. These words of Jesus will change your life. This is both a personal and a present command of Christ for every believer to rest and spend some alone time with Christ. This must become a priority.

> *"Whoever dwells in the shelter of the Most High will rest in the shadow of the Almighty."*
>
> *—Psalm 91:1*

Consider: There are many people in the ministry that find their value by their work in the ministry. They relentlessly work, preach, teach, volunteer, lead, counsel, prepare, clean, visit people, the list can go on and on for the work needed to be done for the ministry. People will work endlessly to build a great, thriving church, business, or finances at the expense of relationships. These 3 words are *"come with me,"* to a place of rest, not *"go do more"* to gain approval.

Challenge: If you are too busy to fulfill these 3 words of Jesus then you are too busy. Meditate on these 3 words of Jesus today and evaluate the time you get away with Him to find true rest. Our greatest call in this life is to intimacy in Christ. Working for Him is not the same as being with Him. The work that we do for the Kingdom should be an overflow of our relationship with Christ. This is because we are filled with the Holy Spirit and motivated by His love; not so we can gain His acceptance or approval.

1. Chambers, Oswald. *My Utmost for His Highest Devotional. Getting There.* June 11th. Retrieved from: https://utmost.org/classic/getting-there-classic/
2. Ibid.

DAY 12

"But with God"

> *Jesus looked at them and said, "With man this is impossible,* ***but with God*** *all things are possible."*
>
> *—Matthew 19:26*

These 3 words of Jesus, *"but with God"* are pivotal for a believer's faith in Christ. To understand what Jesus meant, let's go back to the story of the rich young ruler. This young ruler came to Jesus inquiring about eternal life. Jesus told him to keep the commandments; all which the young man said he had done. Jesus then said that he was lacking one thing. This one thing was keeping him from entering the life he desired. He was to go and sell his possessions, give to the poor, and follow Jesus. This one thing was the idol in his heart. The young man loved his wealth and status. He loved his influence and prestige. This idol was the obstacle to fulfill the call of God in his life. The man went away sad, and likely confused. Culture taught in that time that if a person was rich, they were favored by God and able to accomplish anything they desired. The young man may have walked away wondering how anyone could be saved.

Jesus was not instructing that wealthy people cannot be saved. Jesus was teaching that it is only through Him that people can be saved. Man cannot save themselves through good works, wealth, or obedience to the Law. No one can rely on themselves to save themselves. Jesus' 3 words, *"but with God"* proves that there is nothing impossible with God, including salvation.

Ephesians 2:8-9 says, *"For it is by grace you have been saved, through faith—and this is not from yourselves, it is the gift of God—not by works, so that no one can boast."*

We are limited, God is unlimited. All our strength, wealth, and works are futile to earn salvation or favor with God. If we trust in anything other than Christ for salvation, we fail. We are to rely on His grace, His love and mercy, apart from ourselves, not looking in ourselves. "Well, God knows my heart and I will try and be a good person," does not cut it with God. We are to be conformed to the image of Christ, not allowing the desires of the world and wealth to dominate our first call of loving God. Everything else is an idol.

This young ruler had an idol in his heart that was preventing him from fully entering the life Christ desired for Him. An idol is anything or anyone we place ahead of God in our lives. The desire for money, fame, career, sports, entertainment, family, and success, may be good things, but when the good things replace God's presence in our heart, then things are out of order and need to be re-evaluated. Some idols are clearly sinful, such as, drugs, pornography, greed, and selfishness. These and many others promise fulfillment but only deliver disappointment. Nothing in this life can fulfill the longings of the heart other than Christ.

These 3 words of Jesus, *"but with God"* are to be a reminder that there is nothing impossible with Him. This is about salvation and removing worldly idols that hinder a committed life to Christ. Because *all things are possible with God,* does not mean He gives us all things according to our desires. The closer we align our heart with God, the more His desires will become our desires. God knows what is best for you. We must trust Him to accomplish His will for life because all things are possible with God. Our confidence lies in His ability, not ours.

> *"But you are a chosen people, a royal priesthood, a holy nation, God's special possession, that you may declare the praises of him who called you out of darkness into his wonderful light."*
>
> —*1 Peter 2:9*

⅄⅄⅄

Consider: Are there any idols, or things in your life that are in competition for first place in your heart? Even the *pursuit* of these things; wealth, success, etc., can be an idol. Scripture tells us that, whatever we do, we are to "do it all for the glory of God" (see 1 Corinthians 10:31). Consider the things that your heart longs for and desires. Do you pursue them more than the presence of God in your life? If so, what changes need to be made?

Challenge: Meditate on these 3 words of Jesus, *"but with God."* No one can earn their salvation. No matter what we have or how much money we possess, no one can earn the favor of God, which is received only by His grace. This rich young ruler was fooling himself into thinking he had it all, influence, riches, a moral lifestyle, and respect of the community, but in reality, he had nothing because he did not have Christ. We have nothing if we do not have Christ.

DAY 13

"Watch and pray"

> *"**Watch and pray** that you may not enter into temptation. The spirit indeed is willing, but the flesh is weak."*
>
> —*Matthew 26:41*

Early in the evening Jesus and the disciples finished the "Last Supper" and went out to the Mount of Olives. Jesus tells them, *"This very night you will all fall away on account of me, for it is written: 'I will strike the shepherd, and the sheep of the flock will be scattered.'"* Peter, speaking from his human nature, proudly and boldly proclaims he will not fall away. From there Jesus tells Peter that before the rooster crows, he will have denied Him 3 times. All the other disciples agree that they will never fall away from Jesus. Yet, we know that they all did.

Pride is the gateway to denial. Pride is rooted in all things self. Self-sufficiency, self-serving, self-righteousness all leads to self-deception. Pride is a primary characteristic of self-independence that lives apart from God without concern for others. Pride hides the truth about sin and weakness, often not letting others get to know the real person let alone their struggles. Pride is the source of stubbornness. It has no desire for accountability. It lacks submission. It lacks commitment. No wonder James 4:6 says, *"God opposes the proud but gives grace to the humble."* Dwight L. Moody's words ring true, "God sends no one away empty except those who are full of themselves" (1). Pride idolizes self over God's sovereignty.

Jesus' 3 words, *"watch and pray"* are two powerful commands that are like 2 angelic soldiers guarding the entrance to our mind and heart, continually protecting against the subtle and sudden attacks of the enemy including pride. Jesus' 3 words *"watch and pray"* goes back to when Nehemiah was leading the people in rebuilding the walls of Jerusalem and restoring the gates. The enemy did not want Jerusalem rebuilt, so they used fear, deceit, and every kind of deception to hinder the work. What was Nehemiah's defense? *"Nevertheless we made our prayer to our God, and because of them we set a watch against them day and night"* (Neh. 4:9 NKJV). Watching and praying was the people's defense so they could rebuild the walls and fulfill what God called them to do.

Watching means to keep vigilant and aware. Pride and the flesh are ever seeking to entice and draw you away from His presence and from the duty of prayer. The devil desires nothing more than to turn people away from God. I Peter 5:8-9 *"Be alert and of sober mind. Your enemy the devil prowls around like a roaring lion looking for someone to devour. Resist him, standing firm in the faith, because you know that the family of believers throughout the world is undergoing the same kind of sufferings."* That night in the garden of Gethsemane Jesus knew *what* was coming and Jesus knew *who* was coming. Even in that moment of desperation Jesus was preparing the disciples to understand that in their own strength, in their own humanity and pride, they could never stand against the enemies of Jesus.

These 3 words, *"watch and pray"* that Jesus instructed His disciples and is instructing us today are the "strategy" for victory over temptation. Keep watching for the power and how God is working in your life. Keep praying and seeking further wisdom and guidance from His Word. If we refuse to humble ourselves and obey His commands to watch and pray, we are setting ourselves up for a fall. Jesus in these 3 words gives us the key to victory; be alert and pray.

> *"Therefore, preparing your minds for action, and being sober-minded, set your hope fully on the grace that will be brought to you at the revelation of Jesus Christ."*
>
> *—1 Peter 1:13 (ESV)*

⅄⅄⅄

Consider: Meditate on these 3 words of Jesus throughout your day today. Consider how the Holy Spirit is the source of power, strength and promise that we can depend on to win against our fallen nature, sin, selfishness, and pride. Sin is crouching, ready to destroy your witness, credibility, and the call of God on our lives. Cain stumbled because of pride. Peter opposed Jesus because of pride and earned a divine rebuke. Jesus gives us the key to victory over pride and the flesh – keep watching and praying. If we refuse to humble ourselves and submit to Christ, we will fall.

Challenge: Are there areas of pride, stubbornness, or self-righteousness that you need to submit to God? Meditate on these 3 words of Jesus. Don't let down your guard. The world, the flesh, and the devil are relentless enemies that demand the believer to be alert and in a constant state of vigilance at all times. Dedicate today to *"watching and praying."* Are you dedicated to watching and praying for yourself, your family, your church, and community?

1. Quote retrieved from: https://deeperchristianquotes.com/god-sends-one-away-empty-except-dl-moody/.

DAY 14

"Depart from me"

*"Not everyone who says to me, 'Lord, Lord,' will enter the kingdom of heaven, but the one who does the will of my Father who is in heaven. On that day many will say to me, 'Lord, Lord, did we not prophesy in your name, and cast out demons in your name, and do many mighty works in your name?' And then will I declare to them, 'I never knew you; **depart from me**, you workers of lawlessness."*

—Matthew 7:21-23

Billy Graham famously said, "No man can be said to be truly converted to Christ who has not bent his will to Christ. He may give intellectual assent to the claims of Christ and may have had emotional religious experiences; however, he is not truly converted until he has surrendered his will to Christ as Lord, Savior, and Master" (1).

In this passage, Jesus is speaking of two types of people that will stand before Him, "on that day" (v.22). The phrase "on that day" is the day of judgement, the day when all people will stand before God, and all will be expecting to enter heaven. For some it will be glorious. For others it will be terrifying as Jesus says, *"I never knew you, depart from me."* People will cry out, "we did great things for you, we preached, taught Sunday School, and went on mission's trips for you." Others will say, "We preached powerful sermons, performed healings and cast out demons – all in the name of Jesus!" On that day of judgement many will learn that their investment will yield no return, their "ticket" to heaven is worthless, their "works" did not work. Why? Their works were done for their own glory, not His; for their name and fame not His. Their motivation was to promote their own kingdom and not God's kingdom. His name was used for their personal gain and glory, not for the conversion and discipling of others. Jesus calls them doers of evil and workers of lawlessness. That day will be utterly and unimaginably *terrifying* as Jesus says, *depart from me.*

These 3 words of Jesus speak to the intent of the heart. These people that Jesus will say *"depart from me, I never knew you"* knew *about* Him, but they did not *know Him.* They claimed to have a relationship with Jesus but in reality, there was none. Before everything we do and desire to become in life, we must remember that our first and greatest calling is a personal relationship with Jesus. That is what He desires. John17:3 Jesus says, *"Now this is eternal life: that they know you, the only true God, and Jesus Christ, whom you have sent."*

Matthew uses the term "ginosko" for "knew." Ginosko is a term that describes knowledge based in reality and experience, not speculative or assuming acquaintance. Ginosko is often used to describe an intimate relationship like a married couple. Ginosko comes from living and doing life together, serving together, facing trials, and overcoming them as part of the same team. As Albert Barnes says, "it includes, of course, love, reverence, obedience, honor, gratitude, supreme affection" (2). This is the first call of a believer's life; to know Christ, not as a religious figure but personally and intimately. What a great privilege we have in Christ.

These people to whom Jesus says, *"Depart from me, I never knew you,"* had not lived in harmony with Jesus, and neither did they seek any relationship or intimacy with Him. They were not part of Jesus' team. They did not seek His *kingdom* and His *righteousness* on earth.

How dreadful and terrifying those 3 words of Jesus will be for those people. Commentator Adam Clark soberly sums up these words, "Depart from me —What a terrible word! What a dreadful separation! Depart from ME! from the very Jesus whom you have proclaimed in union with whom alone eternal life is to be found. For, united to Christ, all is heaven; separated from him, all is hell" (3).

True believers are the good trees that produce good fruit, look to Christ, depend on Him, commit themselves to Him, trust in Him, and believe in Him for righteousness, salvation, and eternal life. These are the ones who will enter the kingdom of heaven.

> *"And we know that the Son of God has come, and has given us understanding so that we may know Him who is true; and we are in Him who is true, in His Son Jesus Christ. This is the true God and eternal life."*
>
> —*1 John 5:20*

⅄⅄⅄

Consider: Imagine for a moment the eternal impact and finality of these 3 words. If there were ever 3 words of Jesus that should strike a sober fear into the hearts of people, it would be these 3 words *"depart from me."* Those 3 words will be ringing in the ears for eternity of those who rejected Christ and sought their own fame over building God's Kingdom. Terrifying thought.

Challenge: Meditate on the impact of these 3 words of Jesus. Our first and greatest call is to intimacy with Christ. All works done for God are to be an expression of "ginosko," for the glory of God, salvation, healing, and meeting needs of people. Those who Jesus will say these devastating words to never belonged to Him, they belonged to themselves, they were lord of their own lives, seeking and keeping glory for them and not God. Why do you do what you do? For your glory or God's?

1. quote retrieved from: https://www.preceptaustin.org/colossians_413-18
2. retrievedfromhttps://biblehub.com/commentaries/barnes/john/17.htm
3. Clarke, Adam. "Commentary on Matthew 7:23". "The Adam Clarke Commentary". https://www.studylight.org/commentaries/acc/matthew-7.html. 1832.

DAY 15

"I sanctify myself"

*"For them **I sanctify myself**, that they too may be truly sanctified."*
—*John 17:19*

For the most part, our popular and common idea of sanctification is the progressive riddance of sin in our lives. If we are being sanctified, then we are becoming more holy, removing the lusts of the flesh and the desires of the world, and living at a greater level in the fullness of God. The word *sanctification* is the process of growing toward the holiness of God and away from the sin of the world, conveying the idea of someone gaining holiness and freedom by removing sin from their life.

Then we come across a scripture where Jesus speaks these 3 words *"I sanctify myself,"* is a Jesus sanctifying himself by removing the worldly lusts of the flesh and the carnalities of life and growing spiritually toward God when He says, *"I sanctify myself"*? Absolutely not! The word *sanctification* in this sense is not so much as a *removal from something* as much as it is *dedication to someone*. Jesus lived a completely sinless life dedicated to God and was in no need of sanctification as we understand sanctification. Sanctification is the separation from the world and dedication to the service of God.

The Hebrew word for sanctify is *Qgadosh*. In the Greek it is *hagiazō*. And whether in the Hebrew or whether in the Greek, the words mean the same thing. The words *Qadosh* and *hagiazō* mean to be set aside for the use of

God. Not for common every day uses but for the purposes of God. When Jesus says these 3 words, *"I sanctify myself,"* He is saying, I set myself apart and dedicate myself for the work and purpose of God.

Jesus lived a life dedicated to God. He is the example we aspire to and to whom the Holy Spirit directs. He fulfilled every prophetic scripture written. He suffered and died for our sins and was raised back to life to be seated at the right hand of God. Why would Jesus sanctify himself in this way? The first part of John 17:19 says, *"For them."* That is, for you and me. He brought the knowledge of eternal life to all those who would believe in Him.

John finishes the verse by stating, *"that they too may be truly sanctified."* Jesus is truth and so committed to the mission of God that He willingly laid down His life so that believers can live a sanctified life, dedicated to God by the truth He brought.

Jesus sanctified Himself to reconcile us back to God. Romans 5:10 says, *"For if when we were enemies, we were reconciled to God through the death of His Son, much more having been reconciled, we shall be saved by His life."* His death brought reconciliation to us. His life is a current reality that we do not live *by*, but are to live *in*. His life, His love and power will be continually drawing us to Him and will keep us through until salvation is fully realized. It is for our sake that, *"he is able to save completely those who come to God through him, because he always lives to intercede for them"* (Hebrews 7:25).

These 3 words of Jesus, *"I sanctify myself"* was a powerful demonstration of love for His disciples and for you. Think about it, Jesus lived, loved, taught, even rebuked people – all for us. What a treasure we now have in the Holy Spirit who lives in us. What riches are in the Word of God for our sake. Jesus sanctified Himself so that we may be sanctified. His love is not exclusive, but inclusive, drawing us ever closer to Him and away from the world. This is the desire of God.

The words of Charles Spurgeon give us a great truth to comprehend, "The more truth you believe, the more sanctified you will be. The operation of truth upon the mind is to separate a man from the world unto the service of God" (1). You and I are called to be sanctified; separated, dedicated, and committed to the work of God in our lives and for our lives.

> *"For it is God who works in you to will and to act in order to fulfill his good purpose."*
>
> *—Philippians 2:13*

⅄ ⅄ ⅄

Consider: Jesus' life was dedicated, consecrated, and committed fully to God. He is our example. He inspires us to live a sanctified and dedicated life. His life was sanctified for your life. Consider the sanctification and sacrifice of Jesus for you. How does His sanctified life mold and drive your sanctification and commitment to Christ?

Challenge: Meditate on these 3 words of Jesus. Meditate on the power and purpose that these 3 words bring to you today. Are there any areas of your life that are not dedicated fully to Christ? What about His sanctifying work in your life, what areas are fully consecrated to Him and what areas still need His work? His great love will draw us deeper and closer to Him, and when that happens the lusts, desires and longings for this world will diminish.

1. Quote retrieved from: https://biblehub.com/commentaries/hastings/john/17-19.htm

DAY 16

"But take heart!"

> *"I have told you these things, so that in me you may have peace. In this world you will have trouble.* ***But take heart****! I have overcome the world."*
>
> *—John 16:33*

This verse of Scripture is among the most cherished and one of the most comforting scriptures in the Gospel of John. These 3 words of Jesus, *"but take heart,"* deliver confidence and courage needed to live life. By the death and resurrection of Jesus, He has obtained ultimate victory over this world, and nothing can ever change that. Now, these 3 words are a charge for believers to live in reality of His victory.

Being a Christian does not guarantee an easy life. Jesus did say, *"In this world you will have trouble"* meaning that life will not always be easy. All the disciples, except John were martyred for their testimony of Christ. The early church was often horribly persecuted as Christians were, at times, the target for persecution. No matter what situation you are walking through, or "the cards life has dealt," Jesus says we are to *take heart*. We are to have courage and to rest confidently knowing that Jesus has overcome the world. His victory is our victory. His peace is our peace. His joy is our joy. No trial or tribulation we face can ever change what Jesus accomplished. Reformer Martin Luther wrote, "He (Jesus) does not say: Be comforted, *you* have overcome the world, but this is your consolation, that *I, I* have overcome the world; *my* victory is your salvation" (1).

Jesus gives the key to living and navigating life, *"in me you may have peace."* Jesus again points back to Himself, reminding His followers that He is the Prince of Peace. *"In me,"* is the secret of living life to the fullest. He is what you and I long for and need. We all will experience the pain and pleasures of life. All people are motivated by desire and driven by passion to some degree or another, but what is on the inside will determine what is lived on the outside. If there is turmoil on the inside, life is often in turmoil on the outside. No matter what we face, Jesus says, *"in me you will have peace."*

The possession of peace is one of the greatest spiritual weapons we have. Jesus does not give peace but *offers* peace for the realization and activation found in Him. When the peace of Christ is our possession, there is no situation that can shake our faith, rob our joy, or steal our passion as we live in the reality of these 3 words of Jesus, *"but take heart."* Romans 8 is packed with verses that provide a spiritual reality of Jesus' peace that are to be a reality of life. Here are three of those verses:

- Romans 8:1-2 *"Therefore, there is now no condemnation for those who are in Christ Jesus, because through Christ Jesus the law of the Spirit who gives life has set you free from the law of sin and death."*
- Romans 8:31 *"If God is for us, who can be against us?"*
- Romans 8:37 *"We are more than conquerors through him who loved us."*

This is the work of Jesus in our life if we choose to *take heart*. It is His peace, His victory, His life we are called to live. This will not be found in the outer world, but in the inner reality of His Spirit and life working in ours. Take heart, Jesus has overcome the world, His peace is your peace, His victory is your victory.

> *The Lord gives strength to his people; the Lord blesses his people with peace.*
>
> —*Psalm 29:11*

⅄⅄⅄

Consider: These 3 words give us all we need. Jesus pointed back to Himself as the source for the peace and victory we seek. Consider the work of Christ in overcoming the world. Consider how Jesus is helping you overcome. His Word is alive, active and powerful. What are some other Scriptures that speak strength and peace to you other than the ones above?

Challenge: Meditate on these 3 words of Jesus. Do you *"take heart"* in the reality of Jesus' peace, victory, and life in the circumstance you face? How do these 3 words strengthen your daily life? Spiritual peace does not come from works, service, or things we devote our life to. Spiritual peace comes from Christ, who is the source of peace and the object of faith. This peace is practiced by discovering the greatness of His love, power, Word and fellowship with the Spirit.

1. Quote retrieved from https://biblehub.com/commentaries/meyer/john/16.htm

DAY 17

"Workers are few"

> *"When he saw the crowds, he had compassion on them, because they were harassed and helpless, like sheep without a shepherd. Then he said to his disciples, "The harvest is plentiful but the* ***workers are few****. Ask the Lord of the harvest, therefore, to send out workers into his harvest field."*
>
> *—Matthew 9:36-38*

Pew research is a non-partisan research center that studies trends in society and informs the public about the issues and trends that are shaping the world. In a poll conducted in 2022, they found that, *"Only a few decades ago, a Christian identity was so common among Americans that it could almost be taken for granted. As recently as the early 1990s, about 90% of U.S. adults identified as Christians"* (1).

Wow! Just think about that. 90% of adults claimed to be Christian in the 1990's. The article continues, *"Pew Research Center estimates that in 2020, Christians made up 64% of the U.S. population (including children) while "nones" accounted for 30% and other religious groups 6%. Based on observed data, the baseline scenario assumes that 34% of people who grew up Christian will discard their religion by the time they turn 30"* (2).

In just 3 decades the trend of Christian adults according to Pew went from 90% to approximately 64%. If this trend continues, Christians will make up less than 50% of the population within a couple more decades. These polls do not say it *will* happen, just that the trends say it *could* happen. There are so many reasons and speculations that can be attributed to this alarming decline, but this should make these 3 words of Jesus bring a sober reality to believers today, *"the harvest is plentiful, but the workers are few."*

His comment here meshes with remarks Jesus made after speaking to the woman at the well: *"the fields are white for harvest"* (John 4:35). This is where we come in. Jesus said that we are to ask the Lord of the harvest to send workers into the field. The problem was *not* with the harvest, it is with the harvesters. Throughout the Bible, when the crowds came to Jesus, He was filled with compassion. He met their needs, healed their ailments, and preached the good news. Jesus saw that they were harassed and helpless, like sheep without a shepherd. This is an indictment on the religious leaders of the day because their first duty was to religious rules and regulations and not to seeking the Kingdom of God and helping the hurting.

How are we to activate these 3 words of Jesus and be a harvester? Our first duty is *prayer.* Pray for those in the ministry and the missionaries serving around the world. Secondly, we can *give.* We can give financially or give of your time. Take a new person out to lunch after a church service and build a relationship. Thirdly, we can *share.* Share the love of Christ with someone. There is little doubt that our society needs a move of God. Lastly, we can *lead.* You are a part of this harvest move of God and leading and discipling others is critical. Leading yourself, your family and others is a good place to start. There is always a place in the Church to lead. Christianity may be in decline, but people are searching, people are hurting, and people are in need. People need Jesus. You just might be the miracle they are looking for. What God calls you to, He equips you for.

> *"In the same way, I tell you, there is rejoicing in the presence of the angels of God over one sinner who repents."*
>
> —*Luke 15:10*

⅄ ⅄ ⅄

Consider: Consider these 3 words of Jesus, "*workers are few.*" Maybe you have heard the popular phrase, "God does not call the qualified, He qualifies those He calls." Consider the great leaders of the Bible and who they were when God called them, and then how God used them. God is no respecter of persons, so if God could use these men and women in powerful ways, He can do the same for you.

Think about the decline of Christianity in these past few decades. Along with prayer, giving, sharing, and leading, what part can we play to reverse this trend?

Challenge: Meditate on these 3 words of Jesus. You are an influencer, a harvester, a worker for building the Kingdom of God. How are you impacting the lives of others, especially those in your sphere of influence such as your family, friends, neighbors, and co-workers?

1. https://www.pewresearch.org/religion/2022/09/13/modeling-the-future-of-religion-in-america/
2. Ibid.

DAY 18

"Bread of life"

> *Then Jesus declared, "I am the* ***bread of life.*** *Whoever comes to me will never go hungry, and whoever believes in me will never be thirsty.*
>
> *—John 6:35*

"Watch what you eat!" Have you ever heard these words from a doctor, friend or even yourself? A balanced diet and good nutrition are good for the body and mind. Too much bad nutrition can leave a person feeling sluggish, tired, and sick. Good health requires good nourishment. The same is true of our spiritual lives. Without sufficient intake of spiritual nutrition, our inner being will begin to weaken, affecting our attitude, thought life, prayer life and emotions.

John 6:35 is the first of the "I am" statements in John's Gospel where Jesus states that He is the *"bread of life."* Earlier in the chapter John records that *"a great crowd of people followed him because they saw the signs he had performed by healing the sick"* (v.2). People were following Jesus for what they could get from Him rather than for who He is. They wanted more miracles, more food, and more of the good stuff Jesus offered (v.26). Jesus knew that they were following Him for the wrong reasons. The people were not following Him because their souls were hungry for forgiveness, or because they recognized their need for salvation, but to satisfy their physical appetites and needs.

Jesus was trying to get the people to see the "bigger picture" here. People were living for the temporal; Jesus draws them to the eternal. People wanted food and healing for their fleshly, worldly needs; Jesus was telling them of the greater food and pointing them toward their greatest need; salvation. People were living in the moment; Jesus wanted them to live for the eternal.

It is amazing to think that after Jesus miraculously fed over 5,000 people, they audaciously asked Him to show them a sign to prove He was the Messiah as He claimed. Their argument was that their forefathers had eaten manna from heaven for 40 years, so by comparison Jesus had only done one "meager" miracle with loaves and fish, not daily manna from heaven. What they wanted was for Jesus to give them a free meal again tomorrow. Jesus did not respond to their manipulative efforts. Instead, Jesus said they needed to seek the *"true bread from heaven,"* the One who gives eternal life.

The food and miracles pointed to Jesus as the source of healing and spiritual nourishment. It was not the bread and fish that these people needed but rather to feed on the *bread of life* from heaven. These 3 words of Jesus is a call for believers to examine what nourishes our souls daily.

These 3 words of Jesus are an important challenge to align our loves and priorities. We are driven by what we choose to love. We live for and live out of what we love and express that love with passion, desire, and commitment. What we choose to love in life will dominate the intents of the heart and set the course for life. *1 John 2:17 "The world and its desires pass away, but whoever does the will of God lives forever."* We are not called to live for the temporal, but the eternal.

Our desires, hopes and ambitions are not to be supremely set on the temporal but in the eternal. Our spiritual nourishment is not to come from the things that bring no eternal value. Jesus is the bread of life that satisfies every hunger, drives every desire, and satisfies every longing.

> *Do not love the world or anything in the world. If anyone loves the world, love for the Father is not in them.*
>
> —*1 John 2:15*

⅄⅄⅄

Consider: Consider your personal pursuits between the temporal and eternal. Are you seeking God for who He is or for what He can do for you? Seeking God to only fulfill our needs is not the intent God has for life. Miracles are great, miraculous moves of God are powerful, but they are not to be a distraction from the intimate call of supremely loving God first and foremost.

Challenge: Meditate on these 3 words of Jesus. *Why* do you seek and serve Him? Is it for what He can give or for who He is? Many today are following Jesus for the wrong reason, how are you helping them seek the eternal over the temporal?

DAY 19

"Love one another"

> *"This is my commandment, that you* **love one another** *as I have loved you. Greater love has no one than this: to lay down one's life for one's friends."*
>
> *—John 15:12-13*

It has been said that it is not the *quantity* of our faith we profess that is effective in life but the *quality* of our relationship to Christ that makes the difference. There is a big distinction between quantity and quality. Quantity has to do with amount, quality has to do with a standard or value. A person may say that they have a great amount or quantity of faith and even do great works for the Lord but have no relationship with Jesus whatsoever. Others may not be in the ministry spotlight but have a quality of faith and relationship with Jesus that is deeply and profoundly impactful.

These 3 words of Jesus *"love one another"* are followed by the conjunction *"as."* According to the dictionary, the conjunction, "as" means, "to the same degree," "equally," or "to the same amount" (1). Jesus loved His disciples deeply. The way Jesus loves you is just as profound. Now the command is that they love one another *as,* or to the same degree and according to the same quality to which Jesus loved them.

Jesus' love is the standard to which others are to be loved. This may be a whole lot easier said than done, but people are starving for true, authentic love. Not the love the world says is love, but the love for God that you possess and that is expressed through you. That love brings the hope, healing, and reality of Jesus others are longing for. That love brings glory to God.

So, what does the love of Jesus look like? One way is found in the very next verse in John 15:13, *"Greater love has no one than this: to lay down one's life for one's friends."* His love was a sacrificial love that led Him to the cross to give His life *"as a ransom for many"* (Mark 10:45). Jesus' love is servant-hearted, selfless, unconditional, and sacrificial. His love is good in every way toward us. The word Love used here is the word, *Agape*. Charles Swindoll says, "Agape is the kind of love exemplified by God, especially in relationship with His Son. Moreover, the tense of the verb is present, which suggests repeated or ongoing action: "keep loving one another." The quality of that love must be the same kind as the love we receive from Christ. He is our example and our standard" (2).

Jesus embraced all people, confronted sin, tore down barriers, invited the outcasts and preached a message of love, repentance, and eternal life. His love for people is so great that Jesus, *"for the joy set before him he endured the cross, scorning its shame, and sat down at the right hand of the throne of God"* (Hebrews 12:2). The cross is the greatest demonstration of love. It was joy for Jesus, knowing that the cross was fulfilling God's will, offering salvation, and seating Him at the right hand of the Father. One of the greatest ways we can love others is to lead them to the cross.

Jesus instructs his followers to love in the same way: unconditional, "self-sacrificial", and servant-hearted. His love is our standard for others. There is far too much division, competition, and fighting with one another in Christian circles. We know that this is not harmonious with God's will.

These 3 words of Jesus *"love one another"* seem nearly impossible to demonstrate, but the Holy Spirit will empower us to live as He lived and to love as He loved. Think about it; this world would be revolutionized if believers would love the same way Jesus loved.

Loving others is only accomplished in quality of time and relationship.

Loving others may not be easy and can be complicated, but loving others is found in time, by seeking and pursuing Jesus, in loving Him and being continually filled by His Spirit. We have the chance to love others here and now with a love that is pure and selfless. So, make the most of your moments to love others the way Jesus loves you. It's not about the quantity of love we profess, but the quality of love we possess.

> *"God is not unjust; he will not forget your work and the love you have shown him as you have helped his people and continue to help them."*
>
> *—Hebrews 6:10*

⅄⅄⅄

Consider: When we consider the magnitude of how much Jesus loves us; it is overwhelming. God's love for us is perfect, our love to Him is imperfect, yet Jesus says to *"love others as I have loved you."* He sets the standard of love, not us. The way we can love others is to love God first and foremost with a committed, passionate love.

Challenge: Meditate on these 3 words of Jesus. Maybe you are in a place that you need to be filled with the love of Jesus. That's not a bad place at all. The more you seek and desire to love God, the more you will be filled. Our call is to love others as Jesus loved us. This is a present reality that is demonstrated to the world by receiving His love for us. Are you in a place to receive greater measures of God's love? Are you desperate for God's love?

1. Dictionary.com
2. Swindoll, Charles, Insights on John. Zondervan. Grand Rapids Michigan. 2010. p.243

DAY 20

"I know them"

> *"My sheep listen to my voice;* ***I know them,*** *and they follow me. I give them eternal life, and they shall never perish; no one will snatch them out of my hand.*
>
> *—John 10:27-28*

How amazing are these 3 words of Jesus! Jesus knows those who follow Him. He doesn't just know about them; He knows each one distinctly and intimately. What an amazing thought for each of us personally. God fully knows you. In fact, Jesus knows you as you really are, not the way your family or friends know you or even the way we know ourselves. He sees us as His own – cherished, valued, and loved. These 3 words of Jesus are so profoundly comforting and reassuring that He knows us more deeply than anyone else and He still loves us. This makes us all the more filled with desire to follow Him wherever He leads.

Many, if not most Christians today feel insecure in life. They feel insecure about a job, a relationship, the future, finances, social situations or insecure about their own bodies. Most definitions of insecurity point to a lack of confidence, assurance, and self-doubt. However, the most basic breakdown of insecurity is the *lack of security* or the *lack of feeling safe,* resulting in fear, worry, doubt and uncertainty. One way for each believer to gain a deeper confidence in Christ is to see ourselves, and others through God's standpoint. Psalm 139:13-16 helps us do that:

> *"For you created my inmost being, you knit me together in my mother's womb. I praise you because I am fearfully and wonderfully made; your works are wonderful, I know that full well. My frame was not hidden from you when I was made in the secret place, when I was woven together in the depths of the earth. Your eyes saw my unformed body; all the days ordained for me were written in your book before one of them came to be."*

God knew you before the creation of the world. You were not hidden, but fully known by God. Nothing about you is a mistake. God formed every intricate detail of who you are. You are wonderfully made which means you are distinct, separated, and distinguished. You are made wonderfully from the heart of God, intentionally set apart from the world for Him. We need to remind ourselves that as followers of Christ we are His and He knows us. How comforting.

Notice at the beginning of this verse Jesus says, "My sheep listen to my voice." Jesus' sheep personally belong to Jesus. It is the voice of the Shepherd we need to listen to. He is the one that leads beside the still waters and safe pasture (see Psalm 23). There are a lot of other "voices" that seek to capture your attention and captivate the desire of your heart. Some studies have concluded that there can be between 5,000 and 10,000 images, ads, and messages a day that a person is exposed to. Whether that is true or not, every day we are exposed to other "voices" that seek to direct the intent of the heart. We need to be aware of these "voices" – what they are speaking and where they are leading. What influences you is leading you.

Jesus says, "they follow me." When Jesus speaks, we are to listen. He calls, we respond. There is so much comfort in these 3 words, "I know them," because where He leads, we follow and are safe in His care. He knows what is best for us and we trust that knowledge. The desire for following Christ is to flow from love, not fear, religion, duty, or performance.

The result of our intimate following of Jesus and His gift is John 10:28, "*I give them eternal life, and they shall never perish; no one will snatch them out of my hand.*" The focus of this verse is not on life itself but the keeping power of Christ. No one can snatch away those who belong to Christ. Not anyone or anything unless you allow it to. The ultimate security of Jesus' sheep rests with the good shepherd. Eternal security or the perseverance of the saints means that all those who are truly believers will be kept by God's power and will persevere as Christians until the end of their lives, and they will surely live with Christ in heaven forever.

> *You will keep in perfect peace all who trust in you, all whose thoughts are fixed on you!*
>
> —*Isaiah* 26:3

⅄⅄⅄

Consider: Psalm 139 is a powerful reminder that God knows us better than we know ourselves. Jesus is fully aware of who are His. Our call is to *listen to His voice and follow Him.* Paul reiterates this truth in instructing Timothy: "*Nevertheless, God's solid foundation stands firm, sealed with this inscription: "The Lord knows those who are his," and "Everyone who confesses the name of the Lord must turn away from wickedness*" 2 Tim 2:19 (NIV). The truth of following Christ will be turning from evil.

Challenge: Meditate on these 3 words of Jesus. Jesus knows you; how well do you know Him? How is your personal relationship growing and strengthening in Christ? Jesus is our security in this life, and He will provide eternal life for those who follow Him. How real are these 3 words to you? How do these words build your security in Christ? The truth will turn us from evil as we follow Christ.

DAY 21

"Remain in me"

> ***"Remain in me,*** *as I also remain in you. No branch can bear fruit by itself; it must remain in the vine. Neither can you bear fruit unless you remain in me."*
>
> *—John 15:4*

In our fast-paced society, who has the time to sit around and do nothing? There is always something to be done, plans to be made, people to see, or someplace to go. In the popular vine/branch illustration in John 15:1-17, Jesus' 3 words *"remain in me"* tells His followers do not move; do not go anywhere, stay still, stay rooted where you are planted. Succuss in the Christian life is not about doing, it is about being.

I am sure that you have heard the statement that if Jesus *spoke* something one time, pay attention, if Jesus *repeats* something, pay extremely close attention. In John 15:1-17, the NIV version of the Bible records the words of Jesus to *"remain"* 11 times. The New King James Version uses the word *"abide"* 10 times. These 3 words of Jesus are repeated so much to get our attention about the importance of abiding and remaining in Him.

The Greek word for *"abide"* is *meno*, which means *"to remain"* or *"to stay."* Jesus tells His followers to remain connected to the branch. If we are to produce a life of good fruit, a victorious life, a productive and meaningful life, we must remain connected to the Source that gives life and remain there.

I recently heard a preacher say, "Christianity in America seems to be a mile wide and only an inch deep." In a lot of ways this may seem true. Why? Because people are preoccupied, immersed, and engrossed in so many things that draw affections, desires, and time away from the One who calls us to true life. Being busy is not bad, but when our business is prioritized over our calling and intimacy with Christ, then we are out of order.1 John 2:15-17 says:

> *"Do not love the world or anything in the world. If anyone loves the world, love for the Father is not in them. For everything in the world—the lust of the flesh, the lust of the eyes, and the pride of life—comes not from the Father but from the world. The world and its desires pass away, but whoever does the will of God lives forever."*

The lust of the flesh (carnal and physical appetites, inordinate desires), the lust of the eyes (covetousness, envy), and the pride of life (being arrogant, boastful, or prideful) are an intense battleground for believer's that seek to re-order God's intention of love for us. God's intention is to love Him and seek Him first in all things. The lust of the flesh fights against the will of God for your life. The flesh wants to re-order your loves and turn them to seek *self*-first.

Self-pleasure and self-gratification without consideration of consequence are the core of the flesh despite what God desires for your life. Again, this is not to say that we are not to love other "things." Other things of course are to be loved—but God is to be loved above all else. The call of every believer is to love God foremost, without rivals or challengers.

Notice that John says that the love of the Father is *not in the loves* of the world. John Piper says, "Love for the world pushes out love for God, and love for God pushes out love for the world" (1). The battle for every believer is over their loves and desires. God wants you to love Him and desire Him first and foremost, and the world wants you to love and desire all it offers more than God. British theologian Brooke Westcott wrote, "Whatever is treated as complete without reference to God is so far a rival to God... There can be but one supreme object of moral devotion" (2). There is to be one object of love, desire, and devotion: no rivals, no competitors. That is to be God. The loves of the world are a rival to the love of God. This is the battle we face.

These 3 words of Jesus imply that we are to remain connected to Jesus as the source of life for every area of our life. As we abide, we are further established in His love and our lives express that intimate connection. If there is to be a greater realization of this wondrous relationship, we must follow the words of Psalm 46:10 *"Be still and know that I am God."*

The context of Psalm 46:10 is written for the nation of Israel at a time when they are facing many enemies, but the application of this verse applies today. To *"be still"* is an act of surrender – surrendering one's will, striving, worry and anxiety in exchange for God's peace, wisdom, and direction. God was calling Israel then, and Jesus is calling believers now to "remain," to "abide" in Him by surrendering our worries and strife and to faithfully trust Him as our source of strength and spiritual nourishment.

Jesus' 3 words, *"remain in me,"* is a daily requirement to stay put, do not go anywhere, be still and prioritize the presence of Jesus over all the other things that pull at your heart. The more we learn to draw from Him, the deeper our roots will be in Him, the more our lives will reflect Him.

> *"So then, just as you received Christ Jesus as Lord, continue to live your lives in him, rooted and built up in him, strengthened in the faith as you were taught, and overflowing with thankfulness."*
>
> —Colossians 2:6-7

⅄⅄⅄

Consider: Have you ever really thought about what a privilege it is to be established in Christ? Do we realize the depth of intimate fellowship, the wondrous oneness of life and fellowship He invites us into when Jesus spoke those 3 words, *'remain in me?'*

Challenge: Meditate on these 3 words of Jesus. Has business, ambition, or the drive for other things had a greater priority in your life and moved you away from Christ? If Jesus tells us the importance of remaining in Him, we need to listen.

1. Piper, John. *Do Not Love the World.* Desiring God. https://www.desiringgod.org/messages/do-not-love-the-world. March 10, 1985.
2. Westcott, Brooke Foss. *The Epistles of Saint John*. MacMillan and Co. London. (1892). p.63.

DAY 22

"Feed my sheep"

> *The third time he said to him, "Simon son of John, do you love me?" Peter was hurt because Jesus asked him the third time, "Do you love me?" He said, "Lord, you know all things; you know that I love you." Jesus said,* ***"feed my sheep"****.*
>
> —*John 21:17*

In John 21:15-17 we see Jesus as the Good Shepherd restoring and reinstating Peter. Three times Jesus asks Peter, *"Do you love Me?"* to which Peter responds in the affirmative all three times. The first time Peter tells Jesus, he loves Him, Jesus tells Peter to *"feed my lambs"* (v.15), the second time Jesus tells Peter to *"take care of my sheep"* (v.16) and the third time, Jesus tells Peter to *"feed my sheep"* (v.17).

I think that at some level we all can identify with Peter. How many times have we stumbled, faltered, and denied Christ throughout our Christian journey? In Matthew chapter 18:12-14, Jesus tells a parable of 100 sheep. One sheep wanders off from the fold and is lost. The shepherd leaves the other 99 to find the one that is lost, and when he finds the lost sheep, He greatly rejoices. This brief parable displays the immense love of God for all people and that it is the will of God that none should perish. Before this restoration breakfast, Peter was *the one* of the 99 mentioned in Matthew 18 in need of restoration.

How many times have we re-committed our lives to Christ with a firm resolution to be faithful and committed only to slip away into a spiritual wasteland? We have all been there. We all, in some way or another, relate to Peter. The encouragement for all of us in this passage of John is that Jesus restores His followers to their call even though we stumble at times.

Imagine the burden that lifted from Peter's shoulders when Jesus restores him and assures Him. The guilt of denying Jesus, the self-condemning thoughts, the heaviness of heart that melted away when Jesus spoke those 3 words of affirmation to Peter, *"feed me sheep."* God's purpose and power is greater than any sin we carry. *"Feed my sheep"* is Jesus' charge to Peter. Peter is to be a shepherd who cares for and leads the church. Jesus charges Peter to equip the believers, strengthen the church and seek out other lost sheep still wandering.

Society today is dark and getting darker. What the world needs to see is people who desperately love Jesus. Like Peter, we all are commissioned to feed His sheep. Jesus entrusted Peter to lead, build, guide, and guard His church. These 3 words of Jesus are entrusting *you* to the same call.

Despite Peter's failures and despite our failures, we have a role in the Kingdom of God. Feeding for us means to follow Jesus, love Him and help those in the faith become stronger and more mature. This verse refers to the work of being a shepherd that each believer is called to accomplish. Believers are called to be shepherds of the church, to feed others, share the gospel, nurture, protect the church and go out and get the other 99 that are still lost.

Whether you know it or not you are feeding others. Your words outside of church, your attitudes about the church and actions regarding the church are "food" for others to consume. That's why Paul says, *"conduct yourselves in a manner worthy of the gospel of Christ"* (Phil,1:27). Hebrews 13:7 *"Remember those who led you, who spoke the word of God to you; and considering the result of their conduct, imitate their faith."* We feed and imitate others. Others feed and imitate you. John MacArthur said, "You are the only Bible some unbelievers will ever read" (1). David Jeremiah concurs; "The only Jesus that unbelievers ever see on this earth is the one reflected in those who already know Him" (2). These are some sobering thoughts as to our responsibilities of Jesus' 3 words, *"Feed my Sheep."*

> *"The King will reply, 'Truly I tell you, whatever you did for one of the least of these brothers and sisters of mine, you did for me.'*
>
> *—Matthew 25:40*

⅄⅄⅄

Consider: One of the most powerful displays of this entire passage is how Jesus pursues and restores the fallen. If you are in a place today where you need to be restored to a relationship with Jesus and think, "He would never pursue me," then you don't understand the loving heart of Jesus for His people. Our call is to purpose, not perfection.

Challenge: Meditate on these 3 words of Jesus. Have you allowed failures and disappointments of the past to impede your call to feed His sheep? Failures are a part of life, but they do not determine God's will for you. Are you in a place where you are feeding God's sheep? Keep in mind that Jesus pursues us because He loves us. He restores us because He loves us. He commissions us because He trusts us to love and feed others the way He loves and feeds us. What a great and awesome responsibility we have to work alongside Jesus to restore others and bring others to a deeper faith in Christ.

1. Quote retrieved from; *https://bibleportal.com/*
2. Ibid.

DAY 23

"World may believe"

> *"My prayer is not for them alone. I pray also for those who will believe in me through their message, that all of them may be one, Father, just as you are in me and I am in you. May they also be in us so that the* ***world may believe*** *that you have sent me. I have given them the glory that you gave me, that they may be one as we are one—I in them and you in me—so that they may be brought to complete unity. Then the world will know that you sent me and have loved them even as you have loved me."*
>
> *—John 17:20-23*

In this prayer of Jesus in John 17, Jesus prays for believers to be united *"so the world may believe."* These 3 words of Jesus are part of a prayer that He prayed in the final hours of His life. It is not a prayer for Himself, but a prayer for His disciples, for all believers and even believers today. Jesus prays this prayer from a place of intimate communion and complete oneness with the Father. This place of unity with God is the believer's calling today, to be one with Him in the same way that Jesus and God the Father are one.

Unity is what Jesus prayed for. How can there be unity when there is so much division in the church? Political, doctrinal, and denominational divisions, among many others, are alive and working well and may be one of the reasons that the church seems to have little or no favor in secular society. So where can we begin? What is the key to fulfill the words of Jesus, *"so that the world may believe?"*

John Piper states, "the public effectiveness of our unity is when unbelievers see on the ground attitudes and acts of love among believers" (1). Love is the key. Love is how believers are unified in the Lord. Love is the stamp of authenticity in the Christian faith. Loving God from that place of oneness and expressing that love is the envy of those seeking it. Above the virtues of compassion, kindness, humility, gentleness, patience, and forgiveness; Colossians 3:14 says we are to *"put on love, which binds them all together in perfect unity."* Loving God, loving self rightly, and loving others is the proof of believers dwelling in unity.

Jesus says in this passage that *"they may be one as we are one"* (v.21). Unity with Christ distinguishes believers from non-believers. What non-believers see is our behavior, attitudes, and words. When we pursue unity with Christ, the unbelieving world will take notice. Why? Christians do not act or believe the same as the world. Believers live with peace in the midst of trials, victory over sin, and with a sense of eternal purpose. This unity with Christ is the envy of the non-believer, they just need to realize that your possession can be their reality.

The unity of Christ produces the divine nature we are called to live by. 2 Peter 1:3-4 says, *"His divine power has given us everything we need for a godly life through our knowledge of him who called us by his own glory and goodness. Through these he has given us his very great and precious promises, so that through them you may participate in the divine nature, having escaped the corruption in the world caused by evil desires."* All we have, all we are is because of Christ. He has given us His righteousness so that we may be identified with His love, goodness and grace resulting in our acceptance by the Father through faith in Him.

The purpose of unity with Christ is found in Jesus' 3 words, *"world may believe."* How captivating is the love of Christ. How humbling it is that God has redeemed and reconciled us to Himself and given us this life to live out.

God is good and your life is a message of that goodness so that the *"world may believe"* in God's grace and love.

> *"There is neither Jew nor Gentile, neither slave nor free, nor is there male and female, for you are all one in Christ Jesus."*
>
> —*Galatians* 3:28

⅄⅄⅄

Consider: Consider your role and how the church can demonstrate a greater unity of shared truth, life and hope that can give the lost a reality that Jesus is Lord?

Have you heard the statement of Saint Francis of Assisi, *"It is no use walking anywhere to preach unless our walking is our preaching."* Or another popular statement is, *"You are the only Bible some people will read, you are the only Jesus some people will see."* Believers united in Christ are the light in this world. The Holy Spirit inside of you is the hope others are looking for. Your testimony is one way to express the power of God's love to a broken world. Your testimony of how Christ saved you, healed you, delivered you and loves you. Your testimony is an undeniable reality that no one can take from you. Consider sharing your testimony with others.

Challenge: Meditate on these 3 words of Jesus. Love is the key to fulfilling the mandate of Christ, *"so the world may believe."* It all rests on our personal relationship with Christ. Do you ever think of yourself as so unified with Christ that there is no life to be known apart from life in Him?

1. An interview with John Piper. *Are Divisions in the Church Necessary?* Episode 1746 February 18, 2022. https://www.desiringgod.org/interviews/are-divisions-in-the-church-necessary

DAY 24

"Jesus was amazed pt. 1"

*"**He was amazed** at their lack of faith."*

—*Mark 6:6*

So, today's devotional is not exactly "three words of Jesus" but rather 3 words that are deeply insightful into the heart of God. Scripture records only 2 times when Jesus was amazed, each time the issue was regarding faith. Have you ever wondered what amazes Jesus or how the omniscient Son of God could be astonished by anything? Jesus wasn't impressed by the magnificent buildings in Jerusalem (Matt. 24:12) or standing with powerful political figures (John 19:11). Scripture does not record that Jesus was amazed by art or architecture, human accomplishment, or Rome's military strength. He wasn't impressed by any of those things. He wasn't amazed by power, wealth, or prestige. What did astonish Jesus was *faith*.

The first instance where Jesus was amazed by faith was Mark 6:1-6, *"Jesus left there and went to his hometown, accompanied by his disciples. When the Sabbath came, he began to teach in the synagogue, and many who heard him were amazed.*

"Where did this man get these things?" they asked. "What's this wisdom that has been given him? What are these remarkable miracles he is performing? Isn't this the carpenter? Isn't this Mary's son and the brother of James, Joseph, Judas and Simon? Aren't his sisters here with us?" And they took offense at him.

Jesus said to them, "A prophet is not without honor except in his own town, among his relatives and in his own home." He could not do any miracles there, except lay his hands on a few sick people and heal them. ***He was amazed*** *at their lack of faith."*

When Jesus came back to His hometown of Nazareth, you would think he would get a hero's welcome. After all, Jesus has been preaching the Kingdom of God across the countryside healing the sick, casting out demons, raising the dead, walking on water, and calming storms. Jesus is the talk of the known world, and everyone is coming to Him. When Jesus arrives home and teaches in the Synagogue, the people took offense at him. How could they possibly take offense at Jesus!

Have you ever heard the statements "those who know you best respect you least" or "familiarity breeds contempt?" There were those in Nazareth that knew Jesus, but because of their "familiarity" with Jesus their hearts were filled with unbelief; they are neither convicted nor convinced by His message no matter what miracles He performed confirming His message. Their familiarity with Him was their stumbling block to encounter the Messiah. It astonished Jesus that, despite all the miracles, his townsfolk could see no further than the boy they had grown up with.

Nazareth put Jesus' ministry and life on trial. Warren Wiersbe writes "The contempt shown by the Nazarenes said nothing about Jesus Christ, but it said a great deal about them! A tourist, eager to see everything in the art gallery, fled from picture to picture, scarcely noticing what was in the frames. "I didn't see anything very special here," he said to one of the guards as he left. "Sir," the guard replied, "it is not the pictures that are on trial here—it is the visitors" (1).

The Nazarenes faith was on trial. Except for a few, they were found guilty of having none. Mark uses the word *"skandalizo"* to describe their unbelief. The word means that the Nazarenes were fatally ensnared because of their unbelief *to the point of abandonment*. Seriously? How deep was their familiarity with Jesus as a commoner, a carpenter, and a neighbor that they stumbled over the message and missed the Messiah.

God is never limited, but Jesus refused to perform what He desired to do because of their unbelief. We all will deal with unbelief at times in our life.

There are many personal challenges for us in these 3 words *"he was amazed."* Maybe you grew up in Church, went to Christian school or grew up in a Christian home and you have become so familiar with Jesus that He has lost His wonder. Maybe you have become spiritually numb, frozen in your faith or reeling in your relationship with Christ. If this is the case, then unbelief has taken some territory on your heart and mind. Maybe you are offended and need to deal with the things that caused the "scandal." God wants to amaze you again. Bring your life and faith to Jesus and ask Him to amaze you one more time!

> *"And without faith it is impossible to please God, because anyone who comes to him must believe that he exists and that he rewards those who earnestly seek him."*
>
> —*Hebrews 11:6*

⅄⅄⅄

Consider: How powerful faith is. Faith is what amazed the Son of God. Consider the depth of your familiarity with Jesus. In Matthew 16:13 Jesus asks a profound question to His disciples, *"But what about you?" he asked. "Who do you say I am?"* Who do you say Jesus is? Is He a familiar religious figure or is He the Son of God, the Savior of the world that seeks to captivate your heart?

Challenge: Meditate on these 3 words of Jesus and really think about your faith. Are you too familiar with Jesus? It is amazing to think that the Nazarenes were so offended with Jesus that they would abandon their faith. How would you change familiarity to a deeper faith?

1. Wiersbe, Warren. *Be Diligent; Serving Others as You Walk with the Master Servant. Commentary on Mark.* David C. Cook publishing. Colorado Springs, CO. 1987. p.75

DAY 25

"Jesus was amazed pt.2"

> *"When Jesus heard this, **he was amazed** and said to those following him, "Truly I tell you, I have not found anyone in Israel with such great faith."*
>
> *—Matthew 8:10*

The first time Jesus was amazed was at a lack of faith, and we covered this in yesterday's devotion. The second recording of when Jesus was amazed is at the profound faith of the Roman Centurion who came to Jesus seeking healing for his sick servant. Matthew 8:5-10 records:

> *"When Jesus had entered Capernaum, a centurion came to him, asking for help. "Lord," he said, "my servant lies at home paralyzed, suffering terribly." Jesus said to him, "Shall I come and heal him?" The centurion replied, "Lord, I do not deserve to have you come under my roof. But just say the word, and my servant will be healed. For I myself am a man under authority, with soldiers under me. I tell this one, 'Go,' and he goes; and that one, 'Come,' and he comes. I say to my servant, 'Do this,' and he does it." When Jesus heard this, **he was amazed** and said to those following him, "Truly I tell you, I have not found anyone in Israel with such great faith."*

The faith of the Centurion was not in the belief that Jesus could heal over a long distance. The Centurion's faith was in the realization of Jesus' position of authority. For some time, Jesus was trying to get His followers to understand and believe who He claimed to be – the Son of God. This Roman soldier, who was raised completely outside of the knowledge and covenant promises of God, got it! He understood that Jesus was positioned directly under, and functioned in His Father's authority and all Jesus needed to do was say the word and the servant would be healed. As a man of authority, what Jesus says, got done.

For the Centurion, there was no racial barrier to his faith. He had no problem allowing a Jew to enter his home. Those arguments were irrelevant when it came to his realization of truth. This Centurion realized the truth of what Jesus claimed had been proven by His miracles over sicknesses, diseases, nature and were exemplified in His teachings. The soldier understood authority and the function of authority.

Jesus' commission from the Father was to *"heal the sick, open blind eyes, set free those oppressed and bring salvation"* (Luke 4:18-21). So, when Jesus, under authority of the Father, could just say the word of healing, it would be just as effectual as if Jesus were present to lay hands on the servant. This type of faith the Centurion possessed astonished Jesus. This must have pierced the hearts of Jesus followers as He turned to them and said, *"I have not found anyone in Israel with such great faith."* Ouch! This gentile, Roman Centurion was exhibiting more faith in Jesus than anyone else in Israel. He wanted no outward signs or demonstrations; He wanted just a word.

Jesus has and Jesus is complete authority in and over every situation in life. A Christian's faith is not to be in the work, the healing, or the deliverance that needs to be done, but in the person *Who is* the healer and deliverer. Great faith is understanding that Jesus is the Son of God and to trust wholeheartedly in Jesus despite the situations we experience in life. To understand God's will, we need to understand God's word and abandon ourselves to His love. If we choose to draw close to God, He will draw close to us (James 4:8).

If we draw closer to Him, His Kingdom and authority will draw closer to us. There is so much to be learned about the faith of the Centurion and how his faith can challenge ours to grow.

> *"But when you ask, you must believe and not doubt, because the one who doubts is like a wave of the sea, blown and tossed by the wind."*
>
> *—James 1:6*

⅄⅄⅄

Consider: Consider the faith of the Centurion and the authority of Jesus. The Centurion's faith was great because he penetrated the secret of our Lord's authority and understood exactly where Jesus' authority came from and how it operated.

Challenge: Meditate on these 3 words of Jesus. Compare today's devotional with yesterdays. How is your faith challenged? Are you seeking demonstrations of Jesus or a word from Jesus? Personally, I would like Jesus to be amazed by my belief in His authority, presence, and love, rather than being amazed by my unbelief. How about you?

DAY 26

"More blessed to"

"In everything I did, I showed you that by this kind of hard work we must help the weak, remembering the words the Lord Jesus himself said: 'It is ***more blessed to*** *give than to receive.'"*
—Acts 20:35

In this passage of Scripture, Paul is speaking to the church of Ephesus when he quotes Jesus by saying: *"'It is more blessed to give than to receive.'"* Receiving gifts is not bad at all. Receiving gifts makes a person feel loved and valued, but Jesus is teaching that it is *more* blessed, meaning that there will be more joy and happiness for the person who gives rather than the person who receives. In this passage, Paul sets not only an example for the elders of the church, but also for the followers of Christ. Paul specifically states that we are to work hard to help those who are weak and in need of assistance.

Givers are ultimately people of faith. Giving is an expression of trust, obedience and dependance as believers are freed from the destructive sins of covetousness and greed. Givers do so because they love God and see it as a way to express their devotion. Givers are people of faith because they understand that there are eternal rewards for those who give to advance the Kingdom of God.

1 Timothy 6:18-19 says, *"Command them to do good, to be rich in good deeds, and to be generous and willing to share. In this way they will lay up*

treasure for themselves as a firm foundation for the coming age, so that they may take hold of the life that is truly life." Taking hold of the life that is truly life is focused on personal growth in Christ and prioritizing the Kingdom of God. The only secure investment that can be made is in the Kingdom of God.

Paul writes in Ephesians 3:8, *"Though I am the least deserving of all God's people, he graciously gave me the privilege of telling the Gentiles about the endless treasures available to them in Christ"* (NLT). What are these "endless treasures" that are in Christ? In Christ, *"are hidden all the treasures of wisdom and knowledge"* (Colossians 2:3). In a word: *everything.*

There is no end to God's supply for your life. There is an endless storehouse of resource and blessing; you have everything in Christ. Paul says it is a privilege telling the Gentiles about the treasure Jesus is. Imagine how Paul felt as he was writing these words, and all that Jesus did for him. I bet that Paul was continually overwhelmed with gratitude for the goodness and grace of God, saving him from what he was and conforming him into who he became. Just as Paul's life was an expression of the endless treasure of Christ, so is yours.

Believers are the conduit of God's mercy, love, and grace to the world. Believers are givers, not just receivers – not just finances, but of time and talents as well. The giving believers are called to opportunities for obedience to God as well as opportunities to share the hope we have in Christ. This possession of Christ is the believer's expression. Peter writes, *"His divine power has given us everything we need for life and godliness through our knowledge of him who called us by his own glory and goodness"* (2 Peter 1:3; NIV).

How has God given us everything we need? That treasure is in Christ; knowing God, the Source of all life, is the only path to being fully equipped to live as God calls us to do. These words of Jesus, *"it is more blessed to give than to receive"* strike at the core nature of who we are. There will always be a conflict with the call to give and our nature to receive. When the heart is full of gratitude then it's a joy to give. As followers of Jesus, we have the greatest treasure to give – it is the hope found in Christ.

> *"Command them to do good, to be rich in good deeds, and to be generous and willing to share. In this way they will lay up treasure for themselves as a firm foundation for the coming age, so that they may take hold of the life that is truly life."*
>
> *—1 Timothy 6:18-19*

⅄⅄⅄

Consider: Ephesians 1:3 says, *"Praise be to the God and Father of our Lord Jesus Christ, who has blessed us in the heavenly realms with every spiritual blessing in Christ."* Consider the spiritual blessings God has blessed you with to be a blessing to others. Consider Jesus as our ultimate example; He lived a life of radical generosity, as He demonstrated His compassion in tangible ways: giving sight to the blind, touching the leper, healing the sick, feeding multitudes, and delivering the oppressed. Jesus cared deeply about the poor and the downtrodden.

Challenge: Meditate on these words of Jesus. Are you a giver of time, talents and treasure? Are you a giver of your faith to others? How do these words challenge you personally? How do you handle the treasure that Christ is?

DAY 27

"Father, forgive them"

> *Jesus said, "Father, forgive them, for they do not know what they are doing." And they divided up his clothes by casting lots.*
>
> *—Luke 23:34*

Take a moment and let these 3 words of Jesus sink into your heart; *"Father, forgive them."* Imagine the scenario as the people mocked Jesus, jeered, insulted, pulled out His beard, struck Him repeatedly and ridiculed Him. Imagine the pain of the flogging Jesus endured and carrying His own cross to Golgotha. Imagine the nails being driven into His hands and feet then hoisted between two criminals where people still hurled insults at Him. Imagine this, and yet *forgiveness was in the heart of God.*

Jesus was crucified by the religious leaders because they *hated* him. Imagine the excruciating pain, humiliation and rejection Jesus endured and yet His response was to forgive. *How* could Jesus speak these words and *why* would He speak these words after what He experienced? Only God in His unfaltering love could have spoken these 3 words.

Jesus knew His life's purpose. Romans 5:8-9 says, *"But God demonstrates his own love for us in this: While we were still sinners, Christ died for us. Since we have now been justified by his blood, how much more shall we be saved from God's wrath through him!"* He was conscious that His coming was for a specific purpose—to do the will of the Father. That will, from before the foundation of the world, was the cross, to be the perfect Lamb of God sacrificed for the sins of the world.

On the cross that day, Jesus said, *"Father, forgive them."* Jesus asked for forgiveness for those that put Him on the cross. He prayed for the Roman soldiers that whipped Him, Pilate, the Jewish leaders that accused Him and those that jeered Him. He prayed for forgiveness for every person He was dying for. This included you and me. How powerful and necessary and full of divine grace are these 3 words of Jesus, *"Father, forgive them?"*

Because Jesus spoke these 3 words, you and I were bought with a price (1 Cor.6:20), redeemed and reconciled to God. What a price God paid! Our redemption cost God the life of His Son. Dietrich Bonhoeffer powerfully writes, "what has cost God much cannot be cheap for us. Above all, it is grace because God did not reckon his Son too dear a price to pay for our life but delivered him up for us" (1). This grace of God, the sacrifice of Christ on the cross cannot be cheap to us because it cost God dearly to redeem us. These 3 words of Jesus can change any person's life, if they receive them.

When was the last time someone humiliated or hurt you? When was the last time someone betrayed you that was supposed to love you? All of us will experience pain in this life. If Jesus was rejected and disowned, we will experience rejection as well. We must be careful not to let anger turn to bitterness, or hatred even if we are completely right in the situation. This is always easier said than done, but we have Jesus who understands our pain, betrayal, and rejection. Forgiveness is how we love our enemies, Forgiveness draws us closer to God, Forgiveness releases pain, Forgiveness conquerors.

> *"Get rid of all bitterness, rage and anger, outcry and slander, along with every form of malice. Be kind and tenderhearted to one another, forgiving each other just as in Christ God forgave* you."
>
> —*Ephesians 4:31-32*

Consider: Consider the life, trial, and crucifixion of Jesus. Think about all He endured and yet forgiveness was in His heart. Our society is a fever pitch of being offended by every seemingly small thing. People are offended by books, words, wardrobes and people who have a different opinion than theirs. Being and keeping people offended is unfortunately, an effective tool of the devil.

Challenge: Meditate on these 3 words of Jesus. Are there areas of your life where you are hurt or offended? How can these 3 words of Jesus help you reach the place of forgiving them and gaining greater freedom for you? Mark 11:25 "*And when you stand praying, if you hold anything against anyone, forgive them, so that your Father in heaven may forgive you your sins.*" These 3 words of Jesus are the reason we were redeemed.

1. Bonhoeffer, Dietrich. *The Cost of Discipleship.* Touchstone. 1995.

DAY 28

"It is finished"

*"When he had received the drink, Jesus said, **"It is finished."** With that, he bowed his head and gave up his spirit."*

—John 19:30

With these 3 words Jesus completed His mission set in John 4:34, *"My food," said Jesus, "is to do the will of him who sent me and to finish his work."* These 3 words were so powerful that when Jesus said them every requirement of God's righteous law had been satisfied; God's holy wrath against sin had been appeased, the perfect sacrifice is complete and all that was needed for man's salvation was now accomplished. Man was reconciled to God, enmity between God and man was removed and heaven opened to every believing soul. With these 3 words, Jesus fulfilled every prophecy and sealed every truth of our redemption. It is so important that we understand the magnitude of these 3 words regarding the finished work of Jesus Christ.

AW Pink writes regarding these 3 words of Jesus: "This was not the despairing cry of a helpless martyr. It was not an expression of satisfaction that the end of His suffering was now reached. It was not the last gasp of a worn-out life. No, it was the declaration on the part of the Divine Redeemer that all for which He came from heaven to earth to do, was now done; that all which was needful to reveal the glorious character of God had now been accomplished; that everything necessary for the putting away of the sins of His people, providing for them a perfect standing before God, securing for them an eternal inheritance and fitting them for it, had all been done" (1).

These 3 words of Jesus are an anchor of faith. His victory on the cross is our victory over every enemy. Paul writes in Colossians 2:13-15: *"When you were dead in your sins and in the uncircumcision of your flesh, God made you alive with Christ. He forgave us all our sins, having canceled the charge of our legal indebtedness, which stood against us and condemned us; he has taken it away, nailing it to the cross. And having disarmed the powers and authorities, he made a public spectacle of them, triumphing over them by the cross."* The cross may have seemed like Satan's triumph, but in reality, the cross was his ultimate defeat. *"Having disarmed the powers and authorities, he made a public spectacle of them,"* is the imagery of a Roman parade. Enemies of Rome would be stripped of all armor and marched through the streets in chains signifying their defeat. In the same way, Satan has been stripped of his authority over us. The cross triumphed, the work is done, the devil is defeated! Spiritual victory is secured, and nothing can change that.

Jesus' words have made a permanent effect. These 3 words of Jesus, *"it is finished,"* are prayed to the Father but need to be realized in our daily life. Jesus accomplished the work; it is our responsibility to appropriate that work to our life daily. The strength to live by faith, to live in fellowship with Christ is realized because He has removed the barriers of sin and shame. Sin now has no right to demand anything of us at any time – ever.

Many people may struggle with guilt, fear, anger, or self-worth over their past and may think that some sort of punishment is deserved. It's especially tough when there is a habitual sin repeated that makes people feel that there can be no lasting victory. The power of these 3 words of Jesus *"It is finished"* means it is finished for eternity, there are no works that can supplement or add to the work accomplished by Christ on the cross. He paid the punishment for past, present, and future failures. It's done! His love for you is infinitely greater than the sin we struggle with.

Martin Luther was one who struggled with his sins. Before his break with the Catholic church, he went to confession every day and was so guilt-ridden by his sins he would almost have gone every hour. On most nights Luther slept well, but he even felt guilty about that, thinking, 'Here am I, sinful as I am, having a good night's sleep.' So, he would confess that. One day the older priest to whom Luther went for confession said to him, "Martin, either find a new sin and commit it, or quit coming to see me!" (2).

Christ accomplished it all! Truly He is the good shepherd that lays His life down for the sheep (John 10:11).

> *"For by one sacrifice he has made perfect forever those who are being made holy."*
>
> —*Hebrews 10:14*

⅄⅄⅄

Consider: Consider these 3 words of Jesus and their eternal impact. Consider the fact that there are over 300 prophecies in the OT concerning Christ. He fulfilled every one of them. Consider the payment for sin that Christ became the substitute for, and how those 3 words apply to your faith and relationship to Christ.

Challenge: Meditate on these 3 words of Jesus. How powerful and complete these words are. How do these words affect your personal life and devotion to Christ? Do we truly realize and accept that Christ has paid it all?

1. *Adapted from* The Seven Sayings of the Saviour on the Cross, *6. The Word of Victory, by A.W. Pink. Retrieved from* https://www.preceptaustin.org/john_1930_commentary
2. Illustration retrieved from the Bible Study Notes of John 19:28-30. Retrieved from https://www.calvaryfullerton.org/Bstudy/43%20Joh/1995/43joh19e.htm

DAY 29

"You have seen"

A week later his disciples were in the house again, and – Thomas was with them. Though the doors were locked, Jesus came and stood among them and said, "Peace be with you!" Then he said to Thomas, "Put your finger here; see my hands. Reach out your hand and put it into my side. Stop doubting and believe."

Thomas said to him, "My Lord and my God!"

Then Jesus told him, "Because ***you have seen*** *me, you have believed; blessed are those who have not seen and yet have believed."*

—John 20:26-29

Imagine this scene in John 20. On the first day of the week (v.1), Mary Magdalene, Peter and John go to the tomb where Jesus was laid and found it empty. The disciples leave Mary at the tomb where Jesus appears to her (v.14-17). Mary then goes and tells the other disciples that she has seen the Lord (v.18). That evening the disciples were gathered behind locked doors (v.19), when *"Jesus came and stood among them and said, "Peace be with you! "After he said this, he showed them his hands and side. The disciples were overjoyed when they saw the Lord"* (v19-20).

For some reason, Thomas was not among the other disciples when the resurrected Jesus first appeared to them and *"he breathed on them and said, "Receive the Holy Spirit"* (v.22). The disciples went to tell Thomas what just occurred, and Thomas' response is what secured his title as "doubting Thomas." *"But he said to them, "Unless I see the nail marks in his hands and put my finger where the nails were, and put my hand into his side, I will not believe"* (v.25). It would now be *"a week later* (v.26) before the disciples along with Thomas would gather again. Thomas stewed under the weight of the conversation with the other disciples, *their* experience with Jesus, and *his* questions for a week. I bet he had a few sleepless nights.

Before we are too hard on Thomas, remember that he saw Jesus crucified and saw Him die. Jon Bloom in an article titled *Jesus Helps Our Unbelief* writes, "The slaughter of Jesus outside Jerusalem had been so gruesome that it was all but humanly impossible for Thomas to imagine a resurrection of Jesus's body. True, Thomas had seen Lazarus's resurrection. But Lazarus had died of an illness, and Jesus had been there to raise him. Jesus had been torn to shreds and died" (1). Let's not assume too quickly that we would have responded differently had we seen what Thomas had seen.

Doubt is not the same as unbelief. A person who doubts is questioning what you believe, and what you will place your trust in. Unbelief is outright refusal to believe. There has to be an element of faith in something in order to doubt it. Unbelief is determined resistance. God is not afraid of doubts and questions, in fact, doubts are an invitation into the deeper things of God. Doubts will draw people to seek truth.

Jesus teaches that we are to ask, seek, knock, and the door will be opened to you (Matthew 7:7-8). Keep on asking, seeking, and knocking when those doubts come, (and they will) just choose how you will embrace those doubts. They can drive us into a deeper relationship with God as they did Thomas.

Many today look to other things to supplement their faith like feelings, emotions, even signs and wonders. Believers are called to live by faith in

Christ first. Thomas was a man who had to be sure of his faith, and his questioning of Jesus' resurrection and eventual encounter with Christ secured his hope, faith, and life in Christ for the rest of his life. Thomas' doubt solidified his faith that he eventually became a missionary and brought Christianity to India and was martyred there.

> *"For we live by faith, not by sight."*
>
> *—2 Corinthians 5:7*

⅄ ⅄ ⅄

Consider: There is so much to say about Thomas. All of us will deal with doubts, even the greatest people of faith had their moments where doubt tried to chart a new course and shipwreck their faith. Seeking truth takes time and humility. What are your doubts? How are you dealing with them? Will you allow those doubts to draw you closer to God?

Challenge: These words of Jesus, "***you have seen** me, you have believed; blessed are those who have not seen and yet have believed*" speak directly to us today. None of us has seen the physical body of Jesus, yet Jesus calls us blessed because, despite not seeing what the disciples saw, we believe. The word "believed" carries the idea of a firm and solid faith. We do not need to pretend that we have it all together. Thomas was a man of great faith because his doubts drew him into greater faith. How solid is your belief? How will you strengthen it further?

1. Bloom, Jon. *Jesus Helps Our Unbelief; Moving from Doubt to Delight.* April 4, 2016. https://www.desiringgod.org/articles/jesus-helps-our-unbelief

DAY 30

"I am alive"

> *"When I saw him, I fell at his feet as though dead. Then he placed his right hand on me and said: "Do not be afraid. I am the First and the Last. I am the Living One; I was dead, and now look,* ***I am alive*** *for ever and ever! And I hold the keys of death and Hades."*
>
> —*Revelation 1:17-18*

The resurrection of Christ is by far the single most significant event in human history. This event is the culmination of God's work on the cross and the bedrock of our faith. The resurrection of Christ is an undeniable and understandable demonstration of God's love for all mankind. The resurrection shows that we matter to God. These 3 words of Jesus, *"I am alive"* assures us of God's comfort, forgiveness, and hope of eternal life.

W.E. Vine famously wrote, "By the death and burial of His body He came down to our condition; by His Resurrection He raised us to His position" (1). It is often and well said that Jesus paid a debt He did not owe, and we owed a debt we could not pay. Every facet of faith, life and hope lies in these 3 words of Jesus, *"I am alive."* If there is no resurrection, there is no Christian faith. The fact that Christ is risen means that every word recorded in the Bible is authenticated and proven true. Every prophecy written and every claim Jesus spoke is true. Every claim Jesus made about being the Son of God is true for now and eternity. 1 Corinthians 15:3-4 confirms this: "Christ died for our sins according to the Scriptures, that he was buried, that he was raised on the third day according to the Scriptures."

Jesus said to Thomas, *"I am the way and the truth and the life. No one comes to the Father except through me"* (John 14:6). Truth is truth and life is life, the way to experience life is only in Christ. He is not one of many ways, He is the only way. Yes, Jesus lived, but now He is the living One. This is an undeniable truth.

What do these 3 words of Jesus mean for you today? The eternal life which Jesus offers is not some far off promise to be realized one day when we die. His life is revealed in our life as we draw close to Him (James 4:8) and gain heavenly perspectives in our situations and circumstances (Romans 12:2). His nature becomes our nature as we are changed and molded into His image (Romans 8:29).

The life Jesus gives is foremost eternal life. John 10:10 says, *"I have come that they may have life, and have it to the full."* The "full" or "abundant life" is accessed through our faithfulness to Him that produces good fruit (Galatians 5:22). That life is a vibrant, energetic, relationship with Christ that is experienced here and now.

The more faithful we are, the greater we produce good fruit. Our earthly loves, desires and ambitions begin to take on a new meaning as we grow in the trust and knowledge of God.

Eternal life in Christ is for now. Jesus is life. Our life is realized in His life. His life changes our life, and His love changes our loves and desires. The one thing we need to embrace is that Jesus is all about life!

> *"For you granted him authority over all people that he might give eternal life to all those you have given him"*
>
> *—John 17:2*

Consider: Jesus is alive. This is a fact. Jesus' life is not only for us to receive by faith, but to be lived out day by day, moment by moment, and thought by thought. How is His life being realized and lived out in your life?

Challenge: Meditate on these 3 words of Jesus. The fact that Jesus is alive, and the resurrection cannot be disproven is paramount to our faith and responsibility. Meditate on Vines statement, "He came down to our condition; by His Resurrection He raised us to His position." Jesus took our condition of sin, brokenness, and separation to the cross and destroyed it, providing a way for forgiveness and freedom from sin and shame for all who believe.

1. Vine, W. Collected writings of W. E. Vine. Nashville: Thomas Nelson.

DAY 31

"Sheep among wolves"

> *"I am sending you out like* ***sheep among wolves****. Therefore be as shrewd as snakes and as innocent as doves."*
>
> *—Matthew 10:16*

It seems that if you are a professed follower of Christ today, every action, every word spoken, and each decision is under someone's critical microscope. "I thought you were a Christian?" How many times has that condescending phrase been used to condemn a person who fell short of someone else's exceptional moral standards? Believers are called to be the light of Christ and carry His message into this very dark world, because *that is where He is sending us*. Jesus said, *I am sending you out.* Wait a second, I thought it was the job of the Shepherd to protect the sheep, because after, all Jesus does say in John 10:11, *"I am the good shepherd. The good shepherd lays down his life for the sheep"* and that the shepherd will protect the sheep especially from wolves (John 10:12-13).

In this passage Jesus was speaking to the twelve disciples explaining that He was sending them out like sheep among wolves. This unique band of men were to preach the Kingdom like sheep; humble and harmless. These disciples were sent out by Jesus defenseless and innocent into a world that was as vicious as wolves. People would not be kind to the disciples or their message. They would be mistreated, abused, and hurt by other people's words and actions. People would threaten them and even kill them to stop the spread of the gospel message. The contrast was that Jesus equipped the disciples to face those dangers as His "sent out" ones. Jesus tells them, *"...be shrewd as snakes and as innocent as doves."* Jesus admonished the disciples to be wise, careful, and cunning to avoid danger and not fall into the traps that evil people set for them. They were to remain innocent as doves by not taking offense at the actions of others and to remain sober, vigilant and focused on the mission at hand.

The word *innocent* in this passage means "unmixed," or "pure" (1). Believers are to remain "unmixed" with the world and its lusts, desires, passions, and pursuits. The world desperately needs to hear the message of Christ like never before. Believers are called ambassadors of Christ according to 2 Corinthians 5:20. An ambassador is a representative of one kingdom to another. Believers as ambassadors are commissioned to carry the message of the Kingdom bringing hope and health (Proverbs 13:17), the salvation message and discipleship to all nations (Matthew 28:19-20). Jesus is sending His people out as sheep among wolves, but the good news is that Jesus has equipped believers! Through prayer, the Word, fellowship with other believers, training, and worship, believers are powerfully equipped to be the light of Christ in a very dark world.

People may not receive the message we believe and live by. People may reject the message and at times become abusive. How others choose to react does not negate our call to love others and share the gospel message. We are called to be wise, kind and loving, ready to give an answer to those who ask and not be foolish. Paul in Colossians 4:2-6 wrote:

> *"Devote yourselves to prayer, being watchful and thankful. And pray for us, too, that God may open a door for our message, so that we may proclaim the mystery of Christ, for which I am in chains. Pray that I may proclaim it clearly, as I should. Be wise in the way you act toward outsiders; make the most of every opportunity. Let your*

> *conversation be always full of grace, seasoned with salt, so that you may know how to answer everyone."*

Prayerlessness is ineffectiveness. If there is to be any success in sharing the gospel message it must begin with, continue in, and be celebrated in prayer. Paul also admonishes believers in this verse to be wise. Be wise in your actions, and careful in your attitude toward others. Outsiders will dissect every word, looking for a reason to shame, argue or accuse you of being hypocritical or judgmental. Another key verse is found in Proverbs 9:10, *"The fear of the Lord is the beginning of wisdom, and knowledge of the Holy One is understanding."*

The Fear of the Lord skillfully builds a life that bears a good witness of Christ in all areas of life. People need you. They are longing for spiritual fulfillment and meaning which cannot be fully satisfied outside of Christ. Wisdom, prayer and the Fear of the Lord are elemental attributes that keep a believer from ungodly mixture with the world systems as they are sent out by Christ as sheep among wolves.

> *The fruit of the righteous is a tree of life, and the one who is wise saves lives.*
>
> *—Proverbs 11:30*

⅄ ⅄ ⅄

Consider: Consider these 3 words of Jesus. Jesus sent the disciples out as sheep among wolves. Sheep are meek and mild. Wolves are ravenous and ferocious and in the times of Jesus, one of the most common enemies of sheep. Consider how Jesus sent the disciples out and how Jesus now sends you out?

Challenge: Jesus is still sending believers out today as sheep among wolves. However, we are equipped with prayer, the Word, fellowship, and training just to name a few, for success. Evaluate the way Jesus has equipped you and how well you are functioning in effectively sharing the gospel message of Christ.

Stay close to Jesus. Be kind, be loving, but be smart!

1. Strongs Concordance. Retrieved from https://biblehub.com/greek/185.htm.

Made in the USA
Middletown, DE
09 March 2025

72383495R10061